CO____
CHEERFUL
COOKING

TASTY
SUPPER
DISHES

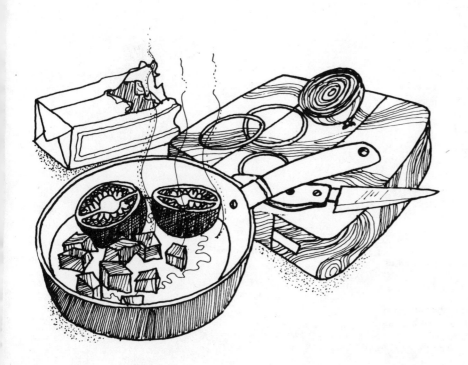

© Wm. Collins Sons & Co. Ltd. 1973
First published 1973
ISBN 0 00 435268 8

Devised, edited and designed by Youé & Spooner Ltd.

Printed in Great Britain by Collins Clear-Type Press

The Publishers gratefully acknowledge the help given
by Allders of Croydon in supplying china and hardware
for use in the colour pictures

COLLINS
CHEERFUL
COOKING

TASTY
SUPPER
DISHES

SUSAN GRAHAM

COLLINS
LONDON & GLASGOW

Useful weights and measures

WEIGHT EQUIVALENTS

Avoirdupois		Metric
1 ounce	=	28·35 grammes
1 pound	=	453·6 grammes
2·3 pounds	=	1 kilogram

LIQUID MEASUREMENTS

$\frac{1}{4}$ pint	=	$1\frac{1}{2}$ decilitres
$\frac{1}{2}$ pint	=	$\frac{1}{4}$ litre
scant 1 pint	=	$\frac{1}{2}$ litre
$1\frac{3}{4}$ pints	=	1 litre
1 gallon	=	4·5 litres

HANDY LIQUID MEASURES

1 pint	=	20 fluid ounces	=	32 tablespoons
$\frac{1}{2}$ pint	=	10 fluid ounces	=	16 tablespoons
$\frac{1}{4}$ pint	=	5 fluid ounces	=	8 tablespoons
$\frac{1}{8}$ pint	=	$2\frac{1}{2}$ fluid ounces	=	4 tablespoons
$\frac{1}{16}$ pint	=	$1\frac{1}{4}$ fluid ounces	=	2 tablespoons

HANDY SOLID MEASURES

				Approximate
Almonds, ground	1 oz.	=		$3\frac{3}{4}$ level tablespoons
Arrowroot	1 oz.	=		4 level tablespoons
Breadcrumbs fresh	1 oz.	=		7 level tablespoons
dried	1 oz.	=		$3\frac{1}{4}$ level tablespoons
Butter and Lard	1 oz.	=		2 level tablespoons
Cheese, grated	1 oz.	=		$3\frac{1}{2}$ level tablespoons
Chocolate, grated	1 oz.	=		3 level tablespoons
Cocoa	1 oz.	=		$2\frac{3}{4}$ level tablespoons
Desiccated Coconut	1 oz.	=		$4\frac{1}{2}$ tablespoons
Coffee—Instant	1 oz.	=		4 level tablespoons
Ground	1 oz.	=		4 tablespoons
Cornflour	1 oz.	=		$2\frac{1}{2}$ tablespoons
Custard powder	1 oz.	=		$2\frac{1}{2}$ tablespoons
Curry Powder and Spices	1 oz.	=		5 tablespoons
Flour	1 oz.	=		2 level tablespoons
Gelatine, powdered	1 oz.	=		$2\frac{1}{2}$ tablespoons
Rice, uncooked	1 oz.	=		$1\frac{1}{2}$ tablespoons
Sugar, caster and granulated	1 oz.	=		2 tablespoons
Icing sugar	1 oz.	=		$2\frac{1}{2}$ tablespoons
Syrup	1 oz.	=		1 tablespoon
Yeast, granulated	1 oz.	=		1 level tablespoon

AMERICAN MEASURES

16	fluid ounces	=	1 American pint
8	fluid ounces	=	1 American standard cup
0·50	fluid ounces	=	1 American tablespoon (slightly smaller than British Standards Institute tablespoon)
0·16	fluid ounces	=	1 American teaspoon

AUSTRALIAN MEASURES
(Cup, Spoon and Liquid Measures)

These are the measures in everyday use in the Australian family kitchen. The spoon measures listed below are from the ordinary household cutlery set.

CUP MEASURES

(Using the 8-liquid-ounce cup measure)

1 cup flour	4 oz.
1 cup sugar *(crystal or caster)*	8 oz.
1 cup icing sugar *(free from lumps)*	5 oz.
1 cup shortening *(butter, margarine, etc.)*	8 oz.
1 cup honey, golden syrup, treacle	10 oz.
1 cup brown sugar *(lightly packed)*	4 oz.
1 cup brown sugar *(tightly packed)*	5 oz.
1 cup soft breadcrumbs	2 oz.
1 cup dry breadcrumbs *(made from fresh breadcrumbs)*	3 oz.
1 cup packet dry breadcrumbs	4 oz.
1 cup rice *(uncooked)*	6 oz.
1 cup rice *(cooked)*	5 oz.
1 cup mixed fruit or individual fruit such as sultanas, etc.	4 oz.
1 cup grated cheese	4 oz.
1 cup nuts *(chopped)*	4 oz.
1 cup coconut	$2\frac{1}{2}$ oz.

SPOON MEASURES

	Level Tablespoon
1 oz. flour	2
1 oz. sugar *(crystal or caster)*	$1\frac{1}{2}$
1 oz. icing sugar *(free from lumps)*	2
1 oz. shortening	1
1 oz. honey	1
1 oz. gelatine	2
1 oz. cocoa	3
1 oz. cornflour	$2\frac{1}{2}$
1 oz. custard powder	$2\frac{1}{2}$

LIQUID MEASURES

(Using 8-liquid-ounce cup)

1 cup liquid	8 oz
$2\frac{1}{2}$ cups liquid	20 oz. (1 pint)
2 tablespoons liquid	1 oz.
1 gill liquid	5 oz. ($\frac{1}{4}$ pint)

Metric equivalents and oven temperatures are not listed here as they are included in all the recipes throughout the book.

When using the metric measures, in some cases it may be necessary to cut down the amount of liquid used. This is in order to achieve a balanced recipe and the correct consistency, as 1oz equals, in fact, 28·35gm.

Introduction

Supper time is the great get-together time, whether it is with the family after work or school, or with friends. In this book I've gone out of my way to choose recipes for you that are worthy of the occasion. Some of them can be made in advance, others are quick enough to prepare almost on the spur of the moment and some you can make when you have a little more time on your hands.

I have included a special chapter of easy-to-eat fare, where you'll find special recipes planned for eating round the fire or when all eyes are glued to the television. There is a chapter of more impressive recipes for entertaining and another on suppers that will stand up to the demands of the late homecomer.

The more complicated recipes can be prepared mainly in advance and either reheated or cooked in the oven. Or you can cook them and then freeze them if you are lucky enough to have a freezer. I do this a lot and find it very useful to have some dishes always pre-prepared and available on those days when I am especially tight for time. You will also find many recipes where you can use cans and packets to save you going shopping specially.

As well as writing books and looking after two children and a very busy husband I have a part-time teaching post. Before I was married I was a domestic science teacher until I entered cookery journalism on several leading magazines and newspapers. When I left full-time journalism after 10 years to cope with home and children, I learnt quite a lot of basic truths, as I now found myself practising all I had been preaching in magazines!

I hope that, whatever the occasion, you'll find these supper recipes helpful and appetising.

Susan Graham

Snacks for the late homecomer

All the recipes in this chapter can either be cooked in advance and heated up later or can be kept in the oven without spoiling.

MINESTRONE
(Illustrated on page 18)
Serves 4

2 tablespoons oil
1 small onion, chopped
1 carrot
1 leek
1 stick celery
2 medium potatoes
3oz (75gm) green peas or green beans
8oz (200gm) cabbage
2–3 tomatoes, skinned and sliced
2 pints (approximately 1 litre) stock
1oz (25gm) macaroni
1oz (25gm) haricot beans, cooked
salt and pepper
grated Parmesan cheese

1. Heat oil in a large saucepan and fry onion for a few minutes.
2. Add finely chopped carrot, leek, celery and potatoes. Then add peas or beans and finely shredded cabbage, and tomatoes.
3. Stir in stock and macaroni. Bring to the boil and simmer very gently for 30 minutes.
4. Add haricot beans and cook for a further 10 minutes.
5. Season with salt and pepper.
6. Pour into soup dishes and serve sprinkled with grated Parmesan cheese.

COCK-A-LEEKIE SOUP
Serves 4–6

carcass and giblets of 1 chicken
1 knuckle of veal
4 pints (approximately 2 litres) cold water
salt and pepper
2 cloves
4 leeks
1oz (25gm) rice

1. Put the chicken carcass, giblets and knuckle of veal into a pan with water, seasoning and cloves.
2. Bring to the boil and add sliced leeks.
3. Simmer for 1¾ hours.
4. Remove the carcass and giblets, add rice and cook for about 20 minutes, until rice is tender.

GRATED VEGETABLE SOUP
Serves 4–6

8oz (200gm) carrots
2 onions
2 potatoes
½ turnip
1 stick celery
1oz (25gm) butter
1½ pints (approximately ¾ litre) stock
5 cloves
1 blade of mace
1 bayleaf
1 pinch of mixed, dried herbs
1 teaspoon salt
¼ teaspoon pepper
½ pint (250ml) milk

1. Scrape and grate the carrots and add to skinned and grated onions.
2. Peel the potatoes and turnip and grate them.
3. Scrub and grate the celery; mix all the vegetables together on a plate.
4. Heat the butter in a pan, add vegetables and cook gently for 10 minutes; mix in the stock.
5. Tie the cloves, mace, bayleaf and mixed herbs into a piece of muslin and put into the pan.
7. Add the seasoning. Cover and simmer for 30 minutes.
8. Remove muslin bag and add the milk. Bring soup to the boil and serve hot.

CHICKEN BROTH
Serves 4–6

1 large chicken carcass with
some meat left on it and the
wings
cold water to cover
salt
1 onion, halved
1 chicken bouillon cube
2 teaspoons rice
1 heaped teaspoon chopped
parsley

1. Remove all the flesh from the
chicken, leaving just the wing
pinions.
2. Put into a pan and add water,
salt, onion and bouillon cube.
3. Simmer slowly for 3½–4 hours,
adding more water, if necessary.
4. Strain the broth and let it cool,
then skim the grease from the top.
5. Bring to the boil and add the
rice. Cook until it is tender.
6. Put parsley in the bottom of a
soup tureen and pour the broth
over it.

POT-AU-FEU
Serves 4–6

2lb (1 kilo) chicken joints
2oz (50gm) plain flour
pepper
2oz (50gm) butter
1 can condensed tomato rice
soup
½ soup can water
French bread to serve

1. Dust the chicken with flour
and pepper.
2. Brown in the butter in a large
saucepan.
3. Stir in soup and water.
4. Cover and cook for 45
minutes over a low heat, stirring
often.
5. Serve with big wedges of
French bread.

MEXICAN MINCE
Serves 4

1 tablespoon olive oil
2 onions, chopped
1 garlic clove, crushed
1lb (½ kilo) raw minced beef
2 level tablespoons flour
salt and pepper
1 can (8oz or 200gm) baked
beans
¼ pint (125ml) water
fingers of toast or fried bread

1. Heat oil in a saucepan and
gently fry the onions and garlic
until soft.
2. Add meat and fry until brown.
3. Sprinkle in the flour and stir
well.
4. Add seasoning, baked beans
and water. Bring to the boil, cover
with a lid and simmer gently for
3 minutes, stirring occasionally.
5. Serve with fingers of toast or
fried bread.

MUSHROOM BEEFBURGERS
(Illustrated on page 18)
Serves 4

1 onion
1lb (½ kilo) minced beef
salt and pepper
1 medium can condensed
mushroom soup
6oz (150gm) fresh breadcrumbs
fat for frying
2 tomatoes, quartered

1. Chop onion quite finely and
mix with minced beef, seasoning,
soup and enough breadcrumbs for
the mixture to be not too wet.
2. Divide the mixture into eight
small beefburger shapes and coat
with remaining breadcrumbs.
3. Fry gently in hot fat for about
15 minutes on each side.
4. Garnish with tomato quarters
and watercress and serve with
baked beans.

PICKLEBURGERS
Serves 4

1lb (½ kilo) minced beef
1 tablespoon chopped parsley
1 tablespoon chopped chives
1 onion, finely chopped
salt
freshly ground black pepper
2 eggs
4 pickled gherkins
1oz (25gm) flour
4oz (100gm) bran flakes,
crumbed
oil for frying
1 tomato, sliced

1. Blend minced beef with parsley,
chives, onion and seasoning.
2. Add 1 beaten egg and mix well.
3. Divide the mixture into flour,
flatten each piece out and place a
gherkin on each.
4. Mould the meat pieces
carefully to oval shapes.
5. Coat them in flour, remaining
beaten egg and bran flake crumbs.
6. Deep fry in oil for 6 minutes,
drain and garnish with tomato.

BEEF CHEESE TURNOVERS
Makes 8 turnovers

2 small onions, finely chopped
1oz (25gm) butter
1lb (½ kilo) minced beef
1 tablespoon Worcestershire
sauce
¼ tablespoon each mustard,
garlic salt, basil, paprika
2 tablespoons soft, white
breadcrumbs
4oz (100gm) Danish blue cheese
2 tablespoons soured cream
(optional)
shortcrust pastry made with
12oz (300gm) flour (see Basic
recipes, page 100)

1. Preheat oven to moderately
hot, 400 deg F or gas 6 (200 deg C).
2. Cook onions in melted butter
until tender but not brown. Add
beef, Worcestershire sauce,
seasonings and breadcrumbs.
3. Cook gently until beef is done,
then allow to cool.
4. Mix in crumbled cheese and
soured cream.
5. Divide pastry into eight pieces
and roll each piece into a circle.
6. Place a spoonful of meat
mixture on the pastry, fold circle
over, damp and pinch edges
together, sealing edges with a
fork.
7. Bake in centre of oven for 15
minutes.

BEEF LOAF
Serves 4–6

1½lb (¾ kilo) minced beef
salt and pepper
1 teaspoon dry mustard
2 tablespoons tomato purée
1 tablespoon Worcestershire
sauce
1 egg
1 packet parsley and thyme
stuffing

1. Preheat oven to moderately
hot, 400 deg F or gas 6 (200 deg C).
2. Mix beef, salt, pepper, mustard,
tomato purée, Worcestershire
sauce and egg together, beating
well until evenly blended.
3. Prepare stuffing according to
packet directions and allow to
stand for 10 minutes.
4. Place half the beef mixture in a
greased tin and cover with the
stuffing.
5. Spread remainder of beef
mixture over and press firmly
down.
6. Bake for 1 hour on centre shelf.
7. Turn out and serve hot, or
leave in the tin until cold before
turning out and serving with
salad.

SUPPER BASKETS
Serves 4

1 packet onion and mushroom
stuffing
1 small packet mashed potato
powder
1oz (25gm) butter
1 small can minced beef
1 egg, beaten

1. Preheat oven to moderate to
moderately hot, 375 deg F or gas 5
(190 deg C).
2. Prepare stuffing and potato
powder according to directions.
3. Mix together and beat in the
butter.
4. Pipe four baskets on to a
greased baking tray and bake in
centre of oven for 15 minutes.
5. Heat minced beef and fill the
baskets with it.
6. Brush baskets with egg and
bake for a further 10 minutes.

POTATO AND MINCE PIE
Serves 4

1lb (½ kilo) potatoes, peeled and
grated
1lb (½ kilo) raw minced beef
1 large onion, peeled and
chopped
1 can (8oz or 200gm) tomatoes
1–2 tablespoons chopped parsley
salt and pepper

1. Preheat oven to very moderate,
325 deg F or gas 3 (170 deg C).
2. Pour off any excess water from
potatoes.
3. Mix all the ingredients
together in a bowl, turn into a
shallow, greased, pie dish and
bake in centre of oven for 1¼–1½
hours. Serve hot.

STEAK AND SAVOURY DUMPLINGS
Serves 4

1 can (1lb or ½ kilo) stewed
steak
1 can (6oz or 150gm) condensed
vegetable soup
½ pint (250ml) water
1oz (25gm) margarine or lard
4oz (100gm) self-raising flour
salt and pepper
½ teaspoon mixed herbs

1. Mix steak and soup together,
add water and bring to the boil.
2. Meanwhile, rub margarine or
lard into flour. Add salt, pepper
and herbs and mix to a firm dough
with a little cold water.
3. Drop heaped tablespoonfuls of
dough into the steak mixture,
cover pan and cook gently for
about 10 minutes.
4. Serve piping hot with baked
potatoes.

CORNED BEEF CASSEROLE
Serves 4

**1 can (8oz or 200gm) corned
beef, sliced
1 can (8oz or 200gm) butter
beans, drained
1 can (10oz or 250gm) carrots,
drained
1 can (10oz or 250gm) condensed
mushroom soup**

1. Preheat oven to moderate to
moderately hot, 375 deg F or gas 5
(190 deg C).
2. Put ingredients into a casserole
dish, arranged in layers.
3. Pour the soup over the top
layer and bake in centre of oven
for 30 minutes. Serve hot.

CORNED BEEF SUPPER
Serves 4

**2oz (50gm) flour
1 can condensed mushroom
soup
1 large can corned beef
1 egg
8oz (200gm) breadcrumbs,
toasted
deep fat for frying**

1. Whisk flour into soup until
blended, then stir until boiling.
2. Shred corned beef and mix
with the soup. Spread on to a
plate until cold and firm.
3. Form into sausage shapes and
dip in beaten egg.
4. Coat with breadcrumbs and fry
in deep hot fat until golden
brown. Drain.
5. Serve hot with salad.

APPLE AND PORK BAKE
Serves 4

**4 lean pork chops
12oz (300gm) cooking apples
2oz (50gm) flour
1oz (25gm) dripping
1 onion, sliced
3 cloves
¾ pint (375ml) stock
salt and pepper**

1. Preheat oven to moderate, 350
deg F or gas 4 (180 deg C).
2. Trim chops; peel, core and slice
apples.
3. Coat chops in flour and fry
until brown on both sides in
dripping.
4. Fry onion and turn it into a
casserole with the cloves. Top
with apples and chops.
5. Add rest of flour to pan and
brown over heat, stirring well.
Blend in stock.
6. Pour over chops and season.
7. Bake on centre shelf of oven
for 1½ hours.

NORFOLK PORK
Serves 4

**12oz (300gm) minced pork
1oz (25gm) lard
2 onions, chopped
2oz (50gm) lentils
4 tablespoons soured cream
¼ pint (125ml) water
2 teaspoons marjoram
4 tablespoons tomato chutney
salt and pepper**

1. Preheat oven to moderate, 350
deg F or gas 4 (180 deg C).
2. Fry minced pork in lard until
brown, then remove from pan.
3. Brown chopped onion in the
same pan.
4. Blend in remaining ingredients,
cover and cook in centre of oven
for 1 hour.

KIDNEY TOASTS
(Illustrated on page 17)
Serves 4

**1lb (½ kilo) sheep's kidneys
salt and pepper
¼ pint (125ml) cream
2oz (50gm) flour
1oz (25gm) lard
2 streaky bacon rashers,
chopped
3 tomatoes, sliced
4 rounds of toast**

1. Skin, core and slice the
kidneys. Season well, dip them in
cream and roll them in the flour.
2. Heat lard and fry the kidneys
until cooked through.
3. Add bacon in the last few
moments.
4. Arrange tomato slices round
the edge of a shallow serving
dish.
5. Place toast in base of dish and
pour kidney mixture over.
Garnish with watercress and
serve at once.

AMERICAN GAMMON STEAKS
Serves 4

1 packet sage and onion
stuffing
1 cooking apple, peeled, cored
and diced
1 large can sweetcorn with
peppers, drained
4oz (100gm) butter, melted
1 egg, beaten
salt and pepper
4 gammon steaks

1. Preheat oven to moderate to
moderately hot, 375 deg F or gas 5
(190 deg C).
2. Prepare stuffing according to
directions on the packet.
3. Add apple, sweetcorn, butter,
egg, salt and pepper.
4. Spread over steaks.
5. Parcel each steak loosely in
buttered foil and bake on a tray
in centre of oven for 30–40
minutes. Serve hot.

STUFFED BACON ROLLS
(Illustrated on page 17)
Serves 4

8 back bacon rashers
2 onions
8oz (200gm) mushrooms
2oz (50gm) dripping
3oz (75gm) breadcrumbs
2 teaspoons chopped parsley
salt and pepper
1 egg, beaten

1. Cut the rind off the bacon.
2. Skin the onions, chop with the
mushrooms and fry gently in
dripping.
3. Mix in the breadcrumbs and
parsley.
4. Season well and bind with egg.
5. Spoon a little stuffing on to
each rasher, roll up and secure
with small skewers.
6. Grill on both sides until heated
through and cooked.
7. Serve with potato crisps.

TASTY BAKE
Serves 4–6

1 packet sage and onion
stuffing
4 slices bacon, de-rinded
1 large can baked beans
1 large can potatoes, drained
and sliced
salt and pepper
1oz (25gm) butter

1. Preheat oven to moderately
hot, 400 deg F or gas 6 (200 deg C).
2. Make up stuffing according to
directions on the packet.
3. Line the base of a greased
casserole dish with 2 bacon slices.
3. Cover with a layer of stuffing, a
layer of beans and a layer of
potatoes, seasoning well between
each layer.
5. Repeat with remainder of
ingredients, finishing with
potatoes.
6. Dot with butter and top with
remaining bacon, chopped. Bake
in centre of oven for 25–30
minutes.

BEAN AND BACON SUPPER
Serves 4

6 bacon rashers
1 can (16oz or 400gm) baked
beans
1 large cooking apple, peeled
1 tablespoon black treacle
black pepper
pinch of nutmeg

1. Preheat oven to moderate, 350
deg F or gas 4 (180 deg C).
2. De-rind and cut bacon into
small pieces and put into a
casserole.
3. Add baked beans, chopped
cooking apple and treacle.
4. Stir well, season with black
pepper and nutmeg and cover
with lid.
5. Cook in centre of oven for 30
minutes.
6. Serve with fried croûtons of
bread.

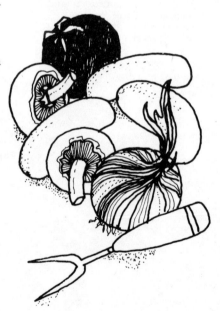

BACON AND MUSHROOM SAVOURIES
Serves 4

1oz (25gm) butter
4oz (100gm) mushrooms, sliced
1 onion, finely chopped
salt and pepper
1 oz (25gm) breadcrumbs
2 level teaspoons chopped parsley
8 streaky bacon rashers

1. Melt butter in a small saucepan and add mushrooms, onion and seasoning. Cover and simmer for 10 minutes.
2. Remove pan from heat and add breadcrumbs and parsley.
3. Remove rind from bacon, stretch each rasher slightly with a knife and spread with mushroom mixture.
4. Roll each rasher up and grill for 5–10 minutes, turning until evenly browned.
5. Serve with baked beans.

SAUSAGES IN MUSHROOM SAUCE
Serves 4

1lb (½ kilo) pork sausages
1 large onion, peeled and diced
2oz (50gm) butter
8oz (200gm) mushrooms, sliced
1 teaspoon mixed, dried herbs
1 teaspoon sugar
1oz (25gm) long-grain rice
salt and pepper
¼ pint (125ml) soured cream

1. Grill or fry the sausages until golden brown.
2. Fry onion in butter for 5 minutes.
3. Add mushrooms, herbs, sugar, rice, salt and pepper.
4. Simmer gently for 10 minutes, then stir in the soured cream.
5. Arrange sausages in a shallow serving dish and pour sauce over the top.

PORK SAUSAGE PIE
Serves 4

1lb (½ kilo) sausagemeat
2 onions
8oz (200gm) tomatoes
2lb (1 kilo) hot, mashed potato
½oz (12gm) butter
salt and pepper

1. Preheat oven to moderately hot, 400 deg F or gas 6 (200 deg C).
2. Put half the sausagemeat into a buttered pie dish.
3. Skin and finely chop the onions and scatter over the sausagemeat.
4. Add the sliced tomato and top with remaining sausagemeat. Season well.
5. Beat the potatoes with the butter and seasoning and fork roughly over the top of the pie.
6. Bake in centre of oven for 45 minutes.

SAUSAGE KIEV
Serves 4

1lb (½ kilo) pork sausagemeat
2oz (50gm) butter or margarine
½ teaspoon mixed herbs
½ teaspoon tomato purée
1 egg, beaten
breadcrumbs
oil

1. Divide sausagemeat into four pieces and flatten into circles.
2. Mix together butter or margarine, mixed herbs and tomato purée and chill in refrigerator.
3. Place a little butter or margarine mixture in centre of each sausagemeat circle.
4. Roll up into balls, brush with beaten egg and coat in breadcrumbs.
5. Fry in hot oil for 10 minutes, then drain and serve with plain boiled rice.

CHICKEN AND POTATO RISSOLES
Serves 4

1lb (½ kilo) potatoes, peeled and boiled
6oz (150gm) chicken, cooked and chopped
1 streaky bacon rasher, fried and chopped
2 large pinches of thyme
½ medium onion, grated
salt and pepper
1 egg, beaten
breadcrumbs for coating

1. Mash the potatoes.
2. Mix the chicken and bacon together and add to the potato.
3. Add thyme, onion, salt and pepper.
4. Stir in half the egg to bind the mixture and form into small, flat cakes.
5. Dip in remainder of egg and coat with breadcrumbs.
6. Fry in shallow fat, on both sides, until golden brown.
7. Serve hot, with green salad or vegetables.

FISH SCRAMBLE
Serves 4

1oz (25gm) margarine
1 level teaspoon curry powder
4 eggs
2 tablespoons milk
salt and black pepper
3–4oz (75–100gm) cooked fish, flaked
4 rounds buttered toast
3 gherkins

1. Melt margarine in a pan, add curry powder and cook for a few minutes.
2. Beat eggs with milk and seasoning and add flaked fish.
3. Pour mixture into the pan and cook gently until mixture begins to thicken, stirring constantly.
4. Remove from the heat and pile on to rounds of buttered toast.
5. Serve at once, garnished with sliced gherkins.

DEVILLED HERRINGS
Serves 4

4 herrings
2 tablespoons mild mustard
2 teaspoons caster sugar
2 teaspoons cider vinegar
a little salt
freshly milled black pepper
2oz (50gm) butter
1 tablespoon browned breadcrumbs

1. Preheat oven to moderate, 350 deg F or gas 4 (180 deg C).
2. Clean and bone the herrings and open out flat.
3. Blend mustard, caster sugar, cider vinegar, salt and pepper together and spread on the herrings.
4. Fold herrings over and arrange them in a buttered dish.
5. Brush liberally with melted butter and sprinkle with the crumbs.
6. Bake in centre of oven for 20 minutes. Serve at once.

YORKSHIRE HERRING PIE
Serves 4

½oz (12gm) butter
1lb (½ kilo) potatoes, peeled and thinly sliced
4 herrings, cleaned, boned and filleted
salt and pepper
½ level teaspoon tarragon
2 teaspoons freshly chopped parsley
1 teaspoon lemon juice
1lb (½ kilo) cooking apples, peeled, cored and coarsely chopped
lemon wedges and sprigs of parsley to garnish

1. Preheat oven to moderate, 350 deg F or gas 4 (180 deg C).
2. Grease a 2½–3-pint (approximately 1¼–1½ litre) casserole dish with butter.
3. Line with half the sliced potatoes.
4. Arrange a layer of herring fillets on top, season and sprinkle with a little tarragon, parsley and lemon juice, and cover with a layer of apple.
5. Repeat the layers, seasoning well.
6. Cook in centre of oven for 45 minutes.
7. When cooked, either turn out on to a serving dish or leave in the casserole dish.
8. Garnish with lemon wedges and sprigs of parsley.

HERRING ROES ON TOAST
Serves 4

8oz (200gm) soft herring roes
2oz (50gm) flour, seasoned with salt and pepper
2oz (50gm) butter
4 rounds of buttered toast
lemon slices and parsley to garnish

1. Wash the roes and dry them.
2. Coat with seasoned flour and fry in hot butter until golden brown and crisp on the outside.
3. Serve the roes very hot on toast, garnished with lemon slices and parsley.

HERRING AND TOMATO PIE
Serves 4

1 medium can herrings in tomato
½ pint (250ml) white sauce (see Basic recipes, page 100)
1oz (25gm) onion, finely chopped
salt and pepper
1lb (½ kilo) cooked, mashed potato

1. Preheat oven to moderately hot, 400 deg F or gas 6 (200 deg C).
2. Drain the herrings and add liquor to white sauce.
3. Stir in onion and salt and pepper to taste.
4. Remove bones from herrings, mash them and add to sauce.
5. Place mixture in a fireproof dish and pipe or fork mashed potato over.
6. Bake in centre of oven for 15 minutes. Serve hot.

PILCHARDS AU GRATIN
Serves 3–4

1 can (1lb or ½ kilo) pilchards in tomato sauce
4oz (100gm) cheese, grated
2oz (50gm) browned breadcrumbs
2 tomatoes, sliced
1oz (25gm) butter

1. Preheat oven to moderately hot, 400 deg F or gas 6 (200 deg C).
2. Turn pilchards and sauce into an ovenware dish.
3. Mix together cheese and breadcrumbs and sprinkle over pilchards.
4. Arrange tomatoes on top and dot with butter.
5. Bake in centre of oven for about 30 minutes until heated through and top is lightly browned.
6. Serve with a green salad.

TUNA MACARONI
Serves 4

1 can tuna fish
1 can condensed cream of tomato soup
4 tablespoons milk
2–4oz (50–100gm) grated Parmesan cheese
3oz (75gm) macaroni
juice of ½ lemon
salt and pepper
2oz (50gm) cheese, grated
brown breadcrumbs

1. Preheat oven to moderately hot, 400 deg F or gas 6 (200 deg C).
2. Drain and flake tuna fish into a basin.
3. Add soup, milk, Parmesan cheese, macaroni, lemon juice and seasoning. Mix together lightly.
4. Turn into a shallow dish and sprinkle on cheese and crumbs.
5. Bake in centre of oven for 25–30 minutes. Serve hot.

CURRIED EGGS
(Illustrated on page 17)
Serves 4

4 hard-boiled eggs, shelled
4 tablespoons cream
salt and pepper
2 level teaspoons curry paste
1 level dessertspoon chutney juice
shake of cayenne pepper
1½oz (37gm) butter
2 small onions, chopped
1 garlic clove
1 level tablespoon curry powder
1oz (25gm) flour
¾ pint (375ml) water
juice of ½ lemon
½oz (12gm) sugar

1. Cut tops off eggs and scoop the yolks into a bowl.
2. Blend with cream, seasoning, 1 teaspoon curry paste, the chutney juice and cayenne pepper.
3. Fill mixture back into egg whites, replace tops and keep eggs warm.
4. Melt butter in a pan and add onions.
5. Crush and add garlic. Cook gently until tender and light golden, but not browned.
6. Mix in remaining curry paste and the curry powder and cook for a few more minutes.
7. Mix in flour and stir over heat until well blended.
8. Add water and season. Simmer for 20 minutes.
9. Blend in lemon juice and sugar.
10. Allow to heat through, then pour over eggs.
11. Serve on a bed of well-seasoned, boiled rice and garnish with chopped red and green peppers.

EGGS IN A BOAT
Serves 4

Hard-boiled eggs served in a hollowed-out crusty loaf, topped with cheese sauce.

4 hard-boiled eggs
1 small crusty loaf in a twist shape
½ pint (250ml) cheese sauce (see Basic recipes, page 100)
1oz (25gm) butter
1oz (25gm) Cheddar cheese, grated

1. Preheat oven to moderately hot, 400 deg F or gas 6 (200 deg C).
2. Slice the hard-boiled eggs.
3. Cut a slice off the top of the loaf lengthways. Hollow out the larger piece and toast both pieces.
4. Add the eggs to cheese sauce.
5. Spread the larger half of the loaf with butter and pour in the cheese and egg sauce.
6. Sprinkle with cheese, replace the 'lid' and put in centre of oven for 15 minutes. Serve with a salad.

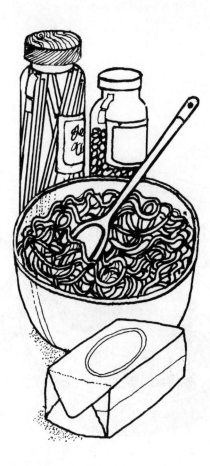

COUNTRY FLAN

(Illustrated on page 17)
Serves 4

shortcrust pastry made with
4oz (100gm) flour (see Basic
recipes, page 100)
2 eggs
¼ pint (125ml) milk
salt and pepper
2oz (50gm) cheese, grated
1 small onion
3 bacon rashers
2 tomatoes

1. Preheat oven to moderate to
moderately hot, 375 deg F or gas 5
(190 deg C).
2. Roll out pastry and line a pie
plate or 7-inch (18cm) flan ring.
3. Break eggs into a bowl and
blend in milk and seasoning. Add
cheese.
4. Chop onion and bacon and fry
gently.
5. Skin and slice tomatoes, place
in the pie case.
6. Add onion and bacon to
tomatoes in pie case and pour egg
and milk mixture over.
7. Bake in centre of oven for 35
minutes.

ONION AND TOMATO FLAN

Serves 4–6

shortcrust pastry made with
6oz (150gm) flour (see Basic
recipes, page 100)
1oz (25gm) butter
2 large onions, sliced
1 egg
¼ pint (125ml) single cream
2oz (50gm) Cheddar cheese,
grated
2 teaspoons chopped parsley
½ teaspoon chopped chervil
½ teaspoon powdered mustard
salt and pepper
4 tomatoes, skinned and
sliced

1. Preheat oven to moderately
hot, 400 deg F or gas 6 (200 deg C).
2. Line an 8-inch (20cm) flan case
with pastry and bake blind in
centre of oven for about 10
minutes.
3. Remove flan case from oven
and reduce oven temperature to
moderate, 350 deg F or gas 4 (180
deg C).
4. Melt butter in a pan, add
onions and fry gently until soft
but not brown.
5. Beat egg with cream, cheese,
herbs, mustard and seasoning.
6. Spread onion evenly in flan
case, add a layer of tomato slices,
pour cream over mixture and
return to oven for 25–30 minutes,
until firm and golden brown.

CHEESE POTATO CAKES

Serves 4

1lb (½ kilo) potatoes
2oz (50gm) cheese, grated
1oz (25gm) butter
½ teaspoon salt
4oz (100gm) flour
2oz (50gm) lard
8 back bacon rashers

1. Peel and boil the potatoes.
2. Drain and mash with cheese,
butter and salt.
3. Sprinkle in the flour and mix
thoroughly.
4. Flatten out in a round and cut
into eight triangles.
5. Heat the lard and cook the
potato triangles until golden on
both sides. Drain and keep hot.
6. Fry the bacon and top each
potato triangle with a bacon
rasher.

MARMALADE CHEESE SNACK

Serves 6

3oz (75gm) butter
4oz (100gm) Cheddar cheese,
grated
4 level tablespoons marmalade
6 slices toast

1. Melt butter in a small
saucepan.
2. Remove from the heat and stir
in grated cheese and marmalade.
3. Place in a small basin and
leave to set.
4. Spread slices of toast with
cheese mixture and grill until
golden brown.

SUPPER LOAF
Serves 4

1 large loaf
6oz (150gm) cream cheese
1 dessertspoon grated onion
paprika
½ cucumber
6oz (150gm) ham, chopped
4oz (100gm) Cheddar cheese,
grated
¾ pint (375ml) white sauce (see
Basic recipes, page 100)

1. Preheat oven to hot, 425 deg F
or gas 7 (220 deg C).
2. Make slits in the loaf at
intervals, taking care that the
cuts do not go through the
bottom crust.
3. Mix cream cheese with onion
and season with paprika.
4. Slice the cucumber and mix
with chopped ham.
5. Fill the slits in the loaf with
these two mixtures.
6. Add half the grated cheese to
the white sauce and heat to melt
the cheese.
7. Place the loaf in a fireproof
dish and pour cheese sauce over
it.
8. Scatter the remaining cheese
over the top and bake in centre of
oven for about 15 minutes.

SUSAN'S SPECIAL
Serves 4

1lb (½ kilo) mashed potato
4oz (100gm) cheese, grated
4oz (100gm) luncheon meat,
sliced
2 eggs, boiled for 6 minutes
1oz (25gm) butter

1. Preheat oven to hot, 425 deg F
or gas 7 (220 deg C).
2. Spread half the potato in a
shallow, ovenware dish.
3. Place the cheese on top, then
add luncheon meat and quartered
eggs.
4. Cover with remaining potato
and mark with a fork or palette
knife.
5. Dot with small knobs of butter
and bake in centre of oven for
about 20 minutes, until browned.

SAVOURY SCONES
Serves 4

8oz (200gm) plain flour
1 teaspoon cream of tartar
½ teaspoon bicarbonate of soda
salt and pepper
½ teaspoon mustard powder
2oz (50gm) butter
4oz (100gm) Cheddar cheese,
grated
¼ pint (125ml) milk
2oz (50gm) cream cheese
tomato pickle
slices of cucumber

1. Preheat oven to moderate to
moderately hot, 375 deg F or gas 5
(190 deg C).
2. Sieve the flour, cream of tartar,
bicarbonate of soda, seasoning
and mustard together in a bowl.
3. Rub in butter until mixture
resembles fine breadcrumbs. Add
cheese.
4. Mix with the milk to make a
soft, elastic dough.
5. Roll out on a floured board
until about ½ inch thick.
6. Using a 3-inch (7·5cm) cutter,
cut out the scones and place on a
floured baking tray.
7. Bake in centre of oven for
about 10–15 minutes until well
risen and browned.
8. To serve, cut in half and top
each with cream cheese, tomato
pickle and a slice of cucumber.

TROPICAL SANDWICHES
Serves 4

4 round slices bread
2oz (50gm) butter
4 slices ham
4 pineapple rings
4oz (100gm) cheese, grated
paprika
parsley to garnish

1. Toast the bread and butter it.
2. Place a slice of ham on each
piece and cover with a pineapple
ring and 1oz (25gm) cheese.
3. Put in a fireproof dish and grill
until golden brown.
4. Sprinkle with paprika pepper
and garnish with parsley.

CHILLI HOTPOT
Serves 4

1 tablespoon oil
2 onions, sliced
1 garlic clove, finely chopped
1 green pepper, sliced
1lb (½ kilo) raw minced beef
1 packet tomato soup mix
¾ pint (375ml) water
1 can (1lb or ½ kilo) red kidney
beans, drained
1½ level teaspoons chilli powder
salt and pepper

1. Heat oil in a saucepan and fry
onion, garlic, pepper and beef
until well browned.
2. Add contents of packet of
tomato soup and water.
3. Bring to the boil and add
kidney beans and chilli powder.
4. Simmer for 30 minutes.
5. Adjust seasoning and serve
with plain boiled rice or creamed
potatoes.

TOMATO TOASTS
Serves 4

1oz (25gm) butter
½oz (12gm) flour
¼ pint (125ml) milk
¼ pint (125ml) sieved tomatoes
or tomato juice
3oz (75gm) cheese, grated
salt and pepper
1 egg
4 slices hot buttered toast

1. Melt butter and mix in flour.
2. Gradually beat in the milk and
tomatoes.
3. Stir well until the mixture
reaches boiling point.
4. Mix in cheese and seasoning.
5. Lower the heat and stir in
beaten egg.
6. Heat through and pour over
slices of toast.

STUFFED TOMATOES
Serves 4

4 large tomatoes
1 teaspoon dried onion
¾oz (18gm) boiled long-grain
rice (raw weight)
salt and pepper
½oz (12gm) butter
1 jar (2oz or 50gm) shrimps
2 tablespoons cooked peas
toast or extra rice to serve

1. Preheat oven to moderate, 350
deg F or gas 4 (180 deg C) if
tomatoes are to be served hot.
2. Cut a slice off the top of each
tomato and scoop out the centres
into a bowl.
3. Add onion, rice and seasoning.
Melt butter in a saucepan add
rice mixture and cook slowly for
about 5 minutes.
4. Stir in drained shrimps and
peas.
5. Pile into the tomatoes and
replace lids.
6. Serve the tomatoes cold with
salad, or bake in centre of oven
for 20 minutes or until tomatoes
are tender.
7. Serve either on toast or with
extra rice.

ASPARAGUS FISH STICKS
Serves 4–5

1 packet (10oz or 250gm) fish
fingers
1oz (25gm) lard
10 asparagus spears, cooked
5 bacon rashers, halved
1oz (25gm) petite Gruyère
cheese, sieved
cayenne pepper

1. Fry fish fingers in lard, on both
sides.
2. When cooked, place an
asparagus spear on each fish
stick and wrap in halved bacon
rasher. Lay in grill pan.
3. Sprinkle with sieved cheese
and cayenne pepper.
4. Grill until cheese melts and
bacon is crisp.

SUPPER SLICE
Serves 4

4oz (100gm) button mushrooms,
sliced
4oz (100gm) streaky bacon,
chopped
1 medium onion, peeled and
finely chopped
1lb (½ kilo) boiled potatoes,
diced
6 large eggs
2oz (50gm) cheese, grated

1. Fry mushrooms, bacon and
onion gently, then add potatoes
and allow to warm through.
2. Beat eggs and pour over the
potato mixture.
3. Sprinkle with cheese and cook
slowly until eggs are set.
4. Brown the top under the grill,
cut into wedges and serve piping
hot.

POTATO MUSHROOM PIE
Serves 4–6

1½lb (¾ kilo) potato, cooked and
sliced
1 onion, thinly sliced
4oz (100gm) cheese, sliced
1 can condensed cream of
mushroom soup
6–8 tablespoons milk or thin
cream
salt and pepper
a little chopped parsley

1. Preheat oven to moderately
hot, 400 deg F or gas 6 (200 deg C).
2. Put potatoes, onion and cheese
in layers in a pie dish, setting
aside enough potato for a final
layer.
3. Mix the soup and the milk or
cream and pour over.
4. Cover with final layer of potato
and season.
5. Bake in centre of oven for
40–60 minutes, until the potato is
cooked.
6. Sprinkle with chopped parsley
and serve with pork chops and
green salad.

FARMHOUSE SPECIAL
Serves 4

1lb (½ kilo) broccoli, cooked and
drained
4 large slices ham
1 can condensed cream of
chicken soup
3–6 tablespoons milk or thin
cream
2oz (50gm) cheese, grated

1. Preheat oven to hot, 450 deg F
or gas 8 (230 deg C).
2. Arrange the broccoli in a
shallow baking dish. Cover with
ham slices.
3. Mix soup and milk or cream
and pour over the ham and
broccoli.
4. Sprinkle with the cheese and
bake in centre of oven for 15
minutes.

Country flan (see page 14)   Stuffed bacon rolls with crisps (see page 10)

Curried eggs (see page 13)   Kidney toasts with tomato slices (see page 9)

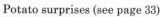

Minestrone (see page 6)   Mushroom beefburgers (see page 7)

Potato surprises (see page 33)   Kipper and egg kedgeree (see page 28)

Fork and finger food

The dishes here can either be pre-prepared or are cooked in individual portions – ideal for evenings when the family doesn't want to move from the fire or a good television programme!

SWEDISH MEAT BALLS
Serves 4

4 onions, chopped
2oz (50gm) butter
8oz (200gm) rump steak, minced
8oz (200gm) shoulder pork, minced
2oz (50gm) white breadcrumbs
1 egg
salt and pepper
¼ teaspoon allspice
¼ pint (125ml) double cream
1 tablespoon water

1. Fry onion in butter until golden brown.
2. Mix all ingredients together and bind well.
3. Make into 1-inch balls, and fry in remaining butter until evenly browned.
4. Shake the pan constantly to keep them round. Drain.
5. Serve hot with a crisp, green salad.

PORK AND APPLE KEBABS
Serves 4

6oz (150gm) pork fillet
1 green pepper, thickly sliced
4 small onions, sliced
4 tomatoes, cut into wedges
2 apples, cored and sliced
4 tablespoons oil
salt and pepper
5oz (150gm) boiled long-grain rice (raw weight)

1. Cut the pork fillet into cubes.
2. Thread meat, vegetables and apple on to four skewers.
2. Combine oil and seasoning and brush kebabs with this mixture.
3. Cook for 10–15 minutes under a hot grill, turning frequently.
4. Serve on a bed of hot rice.

PORK AND PEAS IN A PARCEL
Serves 4

4 pork chops
2oz (50gm) butter
4oz (100gm) mushrooms
juice of half lemon
salt and pepper
8oz (200gm) peas
4 tablespoons cream

1. Preheat oven to very moderate, 325 deg F or gas 3 (170 deg C).
2. Fry chops in butter until browned on both sides. Remove from pan and keep hot.
3. Add sliced mushrooms and lemon juice to the pan. Cook until tender and season well.
4. Put each chop on to a piece of foil measuring about 12 inches across.
5. Top with mushrooms and peas.
6. Add 1 tablespoon cream to each chop, wrap up the foil and bake in centre of oven for 1 hour.

BAKED LAMB FRY
Serves 4

2lb (1 kilo) breast of lamb,
boned
2 onions
2 carrots
salt and pepper
1 teaspoon mixed, dried herbs
½ pint (250ml) water
2 eggs
3oz (75gm) fresh breadcrumbs

1. Preheat oven to very moderate,
325 deg or gas 3 (170 deg C).
2. Lay lamb in a baking dish and
place sliced onions and carrots
over it.
3. Season and sprinkle with
herbs. Add water and cover
closely.
4. Bake in centre of oven for 2
hours.
5. Strain off stock when cooked
and press meat under a weight.
6. When cold, cut into strips, dip
in beaten egg and crumbs and fry
until golden.

MEAT PASTIES
Serves 4

8oz (200gm) plain flour
2oz (50gm) lard
2oz (50gm) butter
salt and pepper
water to mix
4oz (100gm) raw minced meat
4oz (100gm) raw potato,
shredded
1oz (25gm) onion, minced

1. Preheat oven to moderately
hot, 400 deg F or gas 6 (200 deg C).
2. Sift flour and rub in lard and
butter.
3. Add salt and pepper and mix to
a dough with cold water.
4. Roll out and cut into rounds.
5. Mix meat and potato and add
onion and 1 teaspoon water.
6. Season and spoon on to each
pastry round.
7. Seal over and neaten edges.
Bake in centre of oven for 20
minutes.

VEAL AND HAM ROLLS
Serves 4

4 pieces veal escalope
4 slices thin, raw gammon
4 small strips Cheddar cheese
1 egg
breadcrumbs for coating
bacon fat for frying

1. Preheat oven to moderate to
moderately hot, 375 deg F or gas 5
(190 deg C).
2. Lay slices of veal on a board,
with the gammon slices laid on
top.
3. Place cheese at end of each
gammon slice and roll up. Secure
with cocktail sticks.
4. Coat with beaten egg and
breadcrumbs twice.
5. Brown the veal and ham rolls
in ½ inch of hot bacon fat in a
baking tin.
6. Then bake for about 45 minutes
in centre of oven.

SUPPER CROQUETTES
Serves 4

8oz (200gm) cold, cooked beef
or lamb
1 teaspoon chopped parsley
1 teaspoon tomato ketchup
salt and pepper
½oz (12gm) dripping
½oz (12gm) flour
¼ pint (125ml) beef stock
1 egg, beaten
breadcrumbs

1. Mince the meat, removing all
fat, skin and gristle.
2. Mix with parsley, tomato
ketchup and seasoning.
3. Melt the fat, add the flour and
cook for a few minutes.
4. Add the stock and beat over
heat until smooth and well
cooked.
5. Add the meat to the saucepan
and bind the ingredients to a soft
consistency.
6. Turn on to a plate, spread
evenly and leave to cool.
7. Divide into six pieces and
shape into neat cork-shaped rolls.
8. Coat with egg and breadcrumbs
and fry in deep, hot fat.

SUPPER DUMPLINGS
Serves 4–6

4oz (100gm) lamb's liver, finely
chopped
4oz (100gm) bacon, chopped
1oz (25gm) fresh white
breadcrumbs
1 small onion, chopped
1 tablespoon flour
chopped parsley
salt and pepper
1 egg, beaten
1 can kidney soup

1. Mix liver and bacon with
breadcrumbs, then add onion,
flour, parsley and seasoning.
2. Bind mixture with beaten egg
and shape into small balls.
3. Heat the soup in a saucepan.
4. When simmering, add the
dumplings and simmer for about
20 minutes until the dumplings
are cooked.

FAGGOTS
Serves 4

8oz (200gm) pig's liver
4oz (100gm) onions
3oz (75gm) fat pork
1 tablespoon chopped parsley
8oz (200gm) bread, soaked in
water
1 teaspoon mixed herbs
½ teaspoon mixed spice
salt and pepper

1. Preheat oven to moderately
hot, 400 deg F or gas 6 (200 deg C).
2. Mince liver with onions and
pork, then mix with parsley,
bread, herbs and spice.
3. Season very well.
4. Divide into four and wrap each
in greaseproof paper or foil.
5. Bake in centre of oven for 45
minutes. Serve hot.

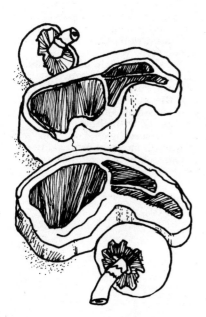

KEBABS ALFRESCO
(Illustrated on page 35)
Serves 4–8

4 lamb's kidneys
1lb (½ kilo) thick rump steak
8 small tomatoes
4oz (100gm) mushrooms
1 small can pineapple slices
1 garlic clove
salt
olive oil
pepper
12 pickled onions
2 medium cans baked beans in
tomato sauce

1. Wash and halve the kidneys,
and cut out core.
2. Cut steak into similar sized
cubes.
3. Wash tomatoes and
mushrooms.
4. Drain pineapple and cut into
sections.
5. Crush the garlic in salt in a
large dish.
6. Pour in sufficient oil to cover
the base, and sprinkle with
pepper.
7. Place all ingredients except
pineapple on the skewers.
8. Marinate in the oil for about 15
minutes, turning the skewers
occasionally.
9. Preheat the grill on the
highest setting, then place
kebabs under for about 4
minutes, turning them
frequently.
10. Reduce the heat, thread the
pineapple on the skewers and
continue cooking for 4–5 minutes.
11. Meanwhile, halve the pickled
onions and heat through in a
saucepan with the baked beans.
12. Arrange the kebabs on top of
the beans and serve immediately.

KIDNEY NESTS
Serves 4

1 egg
1½lb (¾ kilo) mashed
potato
8 lamb's kidneys
1½oz (37gm) butter
2 teaspoons grated onion
1 tablespoon chopped parsley
2 teaspoons made mustard
2 tablespoons tomato pulp
2 tablespoons sherry
1 level dessertspoon flour
parsley to garnish

1. Preheat oven to moderately
hot, 400 deg F or gas 6 (200 deg C).
2. Beat egg into potato and pipe
four potato nests on to a greased
baking tray (or shape with a
spoon).
3. Bake towards the top of oven
until crisp and golden.
4. Meanwhile, skin, core and
slice kidneys.
5. Heat butter in a pan and add
kidney and onion. Cook gently
until cooked and tender, but not
browned.
6. Remove kidney to a plate and
add parsley, mustard, tomato
pulp and sherry to the pan. Stir
well.
7. Blend flour with a little water
and add to the pan. Stir well and
cook for a minute or two.
8. Return kidney to sauce in the
pan and heat through well.
9. Divide kidney mixture between
hot potato nests and serve each
garnished with a sprig of parsley.

SAUTEED KIDNEYS ON TOAST
Serves 4

4 lamb's kidneys
1oz (25gm) butter
1 teaspoon chopped onion
2 mushrooms, chopped
salt and pepper
1 teaspoon flour
¼ pint (125ml) stock
a squeeze of lemon juice
4 rounds of hot toast

1. Skin the kidneys, remove the cores, wash and dry, then slice them.
2. Melt butter and fry onion, mushrooms and add seasoning to taste.
3. Add kidneys and cook, stirring, for about 5 minutes.
4. Mix in flour, then pour in the stock and a little lemon juice.
5. Cook for a few minutes, then serve on toast.

EGG AND KIDNEY FLAN
Serves 4

shortcrust pastry made with 6oz (150gm) flour (see Basic recipes, page 100)
1 small onion
1½oz (37gm) butter
2 lamb's kidneys
1 level tablespoon flour
salt and pepper
¼ pint (125ml) stock or water
6 eggs
1 tablespoon cream
a little chopped parsley

1. Preheat oven to hot, 425 deg F or gas 7 (220 deg C).
2. Roll out pastry and use to line an 8-inch (20cm) flan ring or sandwich tin.
3. Bake blind in centre of oven for 20 minutes. Remove from oven and keep warm.
4. Meanwhile, prepare filling. Chop onion finely and cook gently in ½oz (12gm) butter.
5. Skin and core kidneys and chop up. Add to onion and cook for 2 minutes.
6. Add flour and cook for a further 2 minutes, stirring all the time.
7. Add seasoning and stock or water and simmer for 15 minutes, stirring occasionally.
8. Beat eggs lightly together and season well.
9. Melt remaining butter in a saucepan and pour in eggs. Stir all the time over a low heat until eggs are soft and creamy.
10. Remove from heat and add cream.
11. Place scrambled eggs round sides of flan and kidney mixture in centre.
12. Sprinkle eggs with chopped parsley and serve at once.

SUPPER TOASTS
Serves 4

4 slices bread
1oz (25gm) butter
1 tablespoon chutney
4 slices luncheon meat
4 slices cheese, cut thinly
2 tomatoes
a little made mustard

1. Preheat oven to very moderate, 325 deg F or gas 3 (170 deg C).
2. Toast the bread on one side only. Butter the uncooked side and spread with chutney. Place on a baking tray.
3. Cover with luncheon meat and then cheese.
4. Cook in centre of oven for about 5 minutes, until the cheese begins to melt.
5. Place half a tomato on each, and continue to bake, on the second shelf down, until the tomato is cooked.
6. Top with mustard.

MEAT IN BLANKETS
Serves 4

1 can (7oz or 175gm) luncheon meat
4 bacon rashers, diced
salt and pepper
juice of 1 lemon
1oz (25gm) butter, melted
4 long rolls
chutney

1. Cut meat into 1-inch cubes.
2. Skewer alternate pieces of meat and bacon.
3. Season well and squeeze lemon juice over.
4. Brush with melted butter and grill gently for approximately 10 minutes, turning repeatedly so that the meat cooks.
5. Meanwhile, split warmed rolls and spread with chutney.
6. When meat is cooked, place inside roll and withdraw skewer.
7. Garnish with tomato or watercress.

HOT SAUSAGES AND CHEESE DIP
(Illustrated on page 35)
Serves 4–6

1lb (½ kilo) pork sausages
½ pint (250ml) thick white sauce (see Basic recipes, page 100)
8oz (200gm) cheese, grated
1 teaspoon made mustard
salt and pepper
¼ pint (125ml) cream
4 tablespoons white wine (optional)

1. Twist each sausage into three pieces. Grill until golden and keep hot.
2. Warm the white sauce and stir in the cheese and mustard.
3. Season well and add cream and wine, if used.
4. Spike the sausages on cocktail sticks and serve by dipping them into the sauce.

SAUSAGE AND PEPPER BAKE
Serves 4

4 green peppers
2 tablespoons oil
1 large onion, finely chopped
5oz (125gm) mushrooms, chopped
5oz (125gm) fresh white breadcrumbs
1 level teaspoon mixed herbs
salt and pepper
1 egg, beaten
1lb (½ kilo) pork sausages

1. Preheat oven to moderate to moderately hot, 375 deg F or gas 5 (190 deg C).
2. Cut peppers in half lengthways, remove seeds and blanch in boiling, salted water for 3 minutes.
3. Heat oil in a pan and fry onion and mushrooms gently until tender.
4. Add breadcrumbs, herbs, seasoning and egg and mix well.
5. Fill each pepper with stuffing and arrange with sausages in an ovenware dish.
6. Bake in centre of oven for 25–30 minutes.

SAVOURY SPEARS
Serves 4

4 pork sausages
1 eating apple
2oz (50gm) butter, melted
1oz (25gm) brown sugar
4 bacon rashers
4 tomatoes
4 eggs
3 tablespoons milk

1. Twist each sausage in half.
2. Cut the apple into four and peel and core.
3. Brush with half the butter and sprinkle with sugar.
4. Take the rind off the bacon and roll up each rasher.
5. Thread pork sausage pieces, apple, bacon and tomato on to four skewers and brush with melted butter. Grill until cooked.
6. Put rest of butter into a pan, break in the eggs and add the milk.
7. Stir over a moderate heat until cooked.
8. Turn on to a hot plate with the skewered bacon on top and serve at once.

SAUSAGE NESTS
Serves 4

12oz (300gm) sausagemeat
1 teaspoon finely chopped onion
a little made mustard
2 teaspoons chopped parsley
4 eggs

1. Preheat oven to moderately hot, 400 deg F or gas 6 (200 deg C).
2. Put the sausagemeat into a bowl. Mix in onion, mustard and parsley.
3. Line four individual heatproof dishes with the mixture and bake in centre of oven for 10 minutes.
4. Break an egg into each and return to a moderate oven, 350 deg F or gas 4 (180 deg C) for just long enough to set the eggs.

TELEVISION LOAF
Serves 4

1 onion, finely chopped
1 garlic clove, crushed
12oz (300gm) sausagemeat
1oz (25gm) butter
1 beef stock cube
¼oz (6gm) cornflour
¼ pint (125ml) water
1 tablespoon chopped parsley
1 French loaf, split lengthways
apple slices to garnish

1. Preheat oven to moderate, 350 deg F or gas 4 (180 deg C).
2. Fry onion and garlic with the sausagemeat in melted butter until golden brown.
3. Crush the stock cube and add to the mixture in the pan.
4. Stir in the cornflour and cook gently for 1 minute.
5. Add water, bring to the boil and cook for 1 minute, stirring constantly.
6. Finally, add chopped parsley.
7. Divide the mixture in half and spread on the two halves of bread.
8. Garnish each portion with apple slices, then wrap in cooking foil.
9. Place on a baking sheet and bake in centre of oven for 20 minutes.

NUTTY SAUSAGE CAKES
Serves 4

8oz (200gm) pork sausagemeat
8oz (200gm) mashed potato
salt and pepper
flour
1 egg, beaten
3oz (75gm) chopped walnuts
lard

1. Mix sausagemeat and potato together and season well.
2. With well-floured hands, form into small cakes and dip in beaten egg.
3. Toss in chopped nuts and fry until golden brown in hot, shallow lard. Drain and serve.

SCOTCH EGGS
Serves 4

4 hard-boiled eggs
1oz (25gm) flour
10oz (250gm) sausagemeat
1 egg, beaten
2oz (50gm) fine breadcrumbs
deep fat for frying

1. Shell the hard-boiled eggs, coat with flour and wrap in sausagemeat. (It is important to make sure that there are no cracks in the sausagemeat.)
2. Brush with beaten egg and roll in breadcrumbs.
3. Deep fry in hot, deep fat for about 7 minutes. Drain.
4. Serve hot or cold.

EIGHT O'CLOCK CAKES
Serves 4

6 back bacon rashers
2oz (50gm) medium oatmeal
salt and pepper
pinch of ground ginger
1 egg
6 tablespoons milk
3oz (75gm) bacon dripping
or lard

1. Cut the rinds off the bacon.
2. Put oatmeal, salt, pepper and ground ginger into a small bowl.
3. Add egg and beat well.
4. Stir in the milk and leave mixture to stand.
5. Heat a little dripping and fry bacon rashers slowly on each side until cooked. Keep hot.
6. Heat the rest of the fat in the pan then drop in the oatmeal mixture in tablespoonfuls. Fry slowly on both sides.
7. Serve with the bacon and top with fried eggs, if liked.

BANANA BACON ROLLS
Serves 4

4 back bacon rashers
2 bananas
4 thin slices of bread
2 tomatoes
salt and pepper
butter
parsley

1. Trim and halve the rashers.
2. Peel bananas and cut each into four pieces.
3. Roll each in half a rasher and thread two rolls on each skewer.
4. Toast the bread and halve and season the tomatoes.
5. Grill the rolls and tomatoes and lightly butter the toast.
6. Turn the rolls frequently until they are brown and crisp.
7. Serve on toast on individual plates garnished with tomato and parsley.

BACON-STUFFED TOMATOES
Serves 4

7 streaky bacon rashers
2 rounded tablespoons finely chopped onion
8 large tomatoes
salt and pepper
2 level tablespoons chopped watercress
7 level tablespoons fresh white breadcrumbs
dash of Worcestershire sauce

1. Preheat oven to moderate to moderately hot, 375 deg F or gas 5 (190 deg C).
2. Remove rind from bacon rashers and chop finely.
3. Fry with onion until soft.
4. Cut tops off tomatoes, scoop out centres and seeds and sieve to a pulp.
5. Season the insides of the tomatoes.
6. Mix together the bacon, onion, watercress, breadcrumbs, seasoning, Worcestershire sauce and tomato pulp.
7. Stuff tomatoes with this mixture and replace tomato caps.
8. Bake in an ovenware dish in centre of oven for 20–30 minutes.

HOT HAM CASSEROLE
Serves 4

4oz (100gm) ham, minced
2 tablespoons chilli sauce
1 teaspoon made mustard
1 teaspoon minced onion
1 teaspoon piquant table sauce
1 teaspoon horseradish sauce
6 slices bread, cut thinly
1oz (25gm) butter
3 eggs, beaten
½ teaspoon salt
¾ pint (375ml) milk
3oz (75gm) cheese, grated

1. Preheat oven to moderate, 350 deg F or gas 4 (180 deg C).
2. Mix together ham, chilli sauce, mustard, onion, piquant sauce and horseradish.
3. Spread the bread with this mixture, then place it in a baking dish and dot with knobs of butter.
4. Mix together eggs, salt and milk.
5. Pour over the bread and sprinkle with cheese.
6. Set in a pan of warm water and bake in centre of oven for 1–1¼ hours.

HAM BASKETS
Serves 4

4 bread rolls
3 hard-boiled eggs
8oz (200gm) bacon, cooked
1oz (25gm) butter
1oz (25gm) flour
½ pint (250ml) milk
salt and pepper
1 teaspoon chopped parsley
½ teaspoon made mustard

1. Slice the tops off the rolls and scoop out the insides.
2. Crisp the rolls in oven or under grill.
3. Chop eggs and mince bacon.
4. Melt butter and add flour. Beat in milk; stirring, bring to the boil and season.
5. Add parsley and mustard and mix in eggs and bacon.
6. Spoon into bread rolls and serve hot.

RICE AND HAM SNACKS
Serves 6

6oz (150gm) long-grain rice
1½oz (37gm) butter
1 egg, beaten
3 tablespoons sweet pickle
1 tablespoon chopped parsley
6 slices boiled ham
12 paper-thin onion slices
6 slices tomato
6 slices processed cheese
2 tablespoons grated Parmesan cheese

1. Preheat oven to moderate, 350 deg F or gas 4 (180 deg C).
2. Cook rice in boiling, salted water for about 10 minutes, then drain well.
3. Add butter to cooked rice, then stir in egg, pickle and parsley.
4. Mix well and spoon into a greased ovenware dish. Spread evenly and bake in centre of oven for 10 minutes.
5. Arrange trimmed ham, onion, tomato and processed cheese slices on the baked rice. Sprinkle with Parmesan cheese.
6. Grill just long enough to brown the cheese, then serve immediately.

HAM-RICE PINWHEELS
Serves 4

6oz (150gm) cream cheese
4oz (100gm) boiled long-grain rice (raw weight)
6 green or black olives, finely chopped
1 small onion, grated
1½ tablespoons horseradish cream or relish
1 tablespoon chutney
1 teaspoon Worcestershire sauce
8 thin slices baked or boiled ham

1. Beat cheese until soft and fluffy.
2. Add rice, olives, onion, horseradish, chutney and Worcestershire sauce.
3. Blend well, spread ham slices with rice mixture and roll up tightly.
4. Skewer with cocktail sticks. Cover and chill for several hours.
5. At serving time, cut into 1-inch slices.

CHICKEN TOASTS
Serves 4

4oz (100gm) cooked chicken
4oz (100gm) cooked ham
salt and pepper
sprinkle of nutmeg
3oz (75gm) butter
wedges of toast to serve
watercress
4 tomatoes

1. Mince chicken and ham together twice. Season and add nutmeg.
2. Gradually work in the butter, beat until smooth and spread on hot toast to serve.
3. Top with a sprig of watercress and slices of tomato.

CHICKEN FRIES
Serves 4

8oz (200gm) cooked chicken
½ small onion
1oz (25gm) flour
1½oz (37gm) butter
¼ pint (125ml) milk
salt and pepper
2 eggs
2oz (50gm) breadcrumbs
deep fat for frying

1. Chop chicken fairly finely.
2. Chop onion and put into a frying pan with flour and butter.
3. Cook until tender, but do not brown. Add milk and chicken.
4. Season well and blend in 1 egg. Cook very gently for 3 minutes.
5. Leave to get quite cold and then shape into flat, round cakes on a floured board.
6. Coat in beaten egg and breadcrumbs.
7. Fry in deep fat and drain well. Serve hot.

CHICKEN SHORTCAKES
Serves 4

8oz (200gm) plain flour
4 level teaspoons baking powder
½ level teaspoon salt
1 level teaspoon curry powder
2oz (50gm) margarine or butter
2oz (50gm) cheese, finely grated
¼ pint (125ml) milk
8oz (200gm) cooked chicken meat
half a can condensed chicken soup
2–4 tablespoons single cream

1. Preheat oven to hot, 425 deg F or gas 7 (220 deg C).
2. Sift the flour, baking powder, salt and curry powder into a basin.
3. Rub in the fat until the mixture resembles fine breadcrumbs.
4. Stir in the cheese and add enough milk to mix to a pliable dough.
5. Roll out to ½ inch thick on a floured board and cut into rounds with a 3-inch (7·5cm) diameter cutter.
6. Arrange on a floured baking tray and cook near the top of the oven for 12–15 minutes.
7. Prepare the filling by gently heating the chicken with the soup and adding sufficient cream to give a moist and creamy consistency.
8. To serve, split the warm shortcakes in half and fill with the chicken mixture.
9. Serve hot, garnished, if liked, with bacon rolls and stuffed olives. Serve with a crisp green salad.

CHICKEN BOUCHEES
Serves 4

2 bacon rashers
2oz (50gm) mushrooms
¼ of a roast chicken or 6oz (150gm) chicken meat
½ pint (250ml) thick white sauce (see Basic recipes, page 100)
seasoning
curry powder or grated lemon rind (optional)
1 packet baked bouchée cases (small vol au vent cases)

1. Preheat oven to moderate, 350 deg F or gas 4, (180 deg C).
2. De-rind and chop the bacon and chop mushrooms.
3. Fry both lightly and mix with the roughly chopped chicken meat and white sauce.
4. Season to taste, and add a little curry powder of lemon rind if liked.
5. Pile into bouchée cases and cook on second shelf of oven for about 15 minutes.

HAM AND CHICKEN SURPRISE
Serves 4

1 can ham and chicken roll
2 pineapple rings
1 small packet cream cheese
spread
puff pastry made with 4oz
(100gm) flour (see Basic
recipes, page 100)
1 egg, beaten

1. Preheat oven to hot, 450 deg F
or gas 8 (230 deg C).
2. Cut up the meat roll into
¼-inch dice.
3. Chop pineapple rings and add
to the meat.
4. Add the cream cheese spread
and mix the ingredients together
well.
5. Roll out the pastry to an
oblong, approximately 6 inches by
12 inches.
6. Place the filling down the
centre in a long roll.
7. Damp one long edge of pastry
with beaten egg, roll up and turn
the join underneath. Brush the
top with beaten egg.
8. Using a sharp knife, cut
diagonal slashes along the top of
the roll at 1-inch intervals.
9. Bake in centre of oven for
20–25 minutes, until golden
brown.
10. Serve hot with vegetables or
cold with green salad.

POTTED CHICKEN TOASTS
Serves 4

4oz (100gm) cooked chicken
4oz (100gm) cooked ham
salt and pepper
sprinkle of nutmeg
3oz (75gm) butter
wedges of toast to serve
4 tomatoes
4 sprigs of watercress

1. Mince chicken and ham
together twice. Season and add
nutmeg.
2. Gradually work in the butter.
Beat until smooth and spread on
hot toast to serve.
3. Top with slices of tomato and a
sprig of watercress.

WOODCOCK TOASTS
Serves 4

4 chicken livers, cooked
2 teaspoons anchovy essence
2oz (50gm) butter
2 egg yolks
¼ pint (125ml) cream
buttered toast fingers
chopped parsley

1. Mash chicken livers with
anchovy essence, butter and egg
yolks, then sieve.
2. Add the cream and heat
gently, stirring well, until the
mixture thickens.
3. Spread on hot toast fingers and
garnish with parsley.

DEVILLED TURKEY SAVOURIES
Serves 4

8oz (200gm) cooked turkey
1½ teaspoons curry paste
½ teaspoon mustard
2 teaspoons hot chutney
2 teaspoons mushroom
ketchup
2oz (50gm) butter
4 rounds of fried bread

1. Remove the turkey from the
bones and cut into small pieces.
2. Mix together curry paste,
mustard, chutney, ketchup and
butter and mix with the turkey.
3. Stir over a low heat.
4. When hot, pile on to fried
bread and serve at once.

TURKEY TEMPTERS
Serves 4

Turkey and mushrooms in baked
potatoes.

1lb (½ kilo) cooked turkey,
chopped
8oz (200gm) mushrooms,
chopped
6 tablespoons cream
1 tablespoon chopped parsley
4 hot, baked potatoes
1oz (25gm) butter
chopped parsley to garnish

1. Mix together turkey and
mushrooms with cream and
parsley. Heat very gently.
2. Cut the tops off the hot
potatoes and scoop out some of
the soft inside. Replace with
turkey mixture.
3. Spoon the extra potato round
the dish that the potatoes are
served on and dot with butter.
7. Sprinkle with parsley and
serve.

DUCK IN RED WINE ON TOAST
Serves 4

2 tablespoons butter
2oz (50gm) flour
6 tablespoons red wine
½ pint (250ml) stock
salt and pepper
1 teaspoon chopped onion
1 teaspoon chopped parsley
1 teaspoon grated lemon or orange peel
bouquet garni
slices of cold roast duck
1 duck liver
4 rounds of toast

1. Melt butter and stir in flour.
2. Mix in wine, stock, salt and pepper and stir well until sauce is smooth.
3. Add onion, parsley, grated peel, bouquet garni and duck slices.
4. Cover and simmer gently for 1 hour.
5. Remove bouquet garni and add chopped duck liver.
6. Serve on rounds of toast.

KIPPER AND TOMATO RAREBIT
Serves 4

4 slices bread
1oz (25gm) butter
1 packet frozen kipper fillets, thawed
3 tomatoes, sliced
3oz (75gm) cheese, grated
chopped parsley to garnish

1. Toast both sides of bread.
2. Butter one side. Skin kipper fillets and divide between the 4 slices.
3. Place under grill for 4–5 minutes.
4. Cover with slices of tomato and top with a layer of cheese.
5. Return to grill for a further 3–4 minutes, until cheese has melted.
6. Garnish with parsley.

LEMONY KIPPER SNACK ON TOAST
Serves 4

1 packet frozen kipper fillets, thawed
2 hard-boiled eggs, chopped
½oz (12gm) butter
½oz (12gm) flour
¼ pint (125ml) milk
juice and grated rind of half a lemon
salt and pepper
4 slices hot, buttered toast
2oz (50gm) cheese, grated

1. Chop all but 2 fillets and mix with chopped egg.
2. Melt butter, add flour and blend.
3. Allow to cook gently, then gradually add milk, stirring continuously until thickened.
4. Add grated lemon rind and juice and season to taste.
5. Stir in prepared, chopped kipper and egg and spoon on to hot, buttered toast.
6. Add remaining kipper fillets which have been cut in half and sprinkle with grated cheese.
7. Place under hot grill for about 5 minutes, until golden and bubbling.

KIPPER AND EGG KEDGEREE
(Illustrated on page 18)
Serves 4–6

2 packets frozen kipper fillets
2oz (50gm) butter
6oz (150gm) boiled long-grain rice, well dried (raw weight)
3 hard-boiled eggs
salt and pepper
1 egg, beaten
4–5 tablespoons cream or milk
1 tablespoon prepared English mustard
parsley sprigs

1. Defrost kippers and reserve 2 fillets. Cut rest into big shreds.
2. Melt butter in a pan, add kipper pieces and shake over heat until hot.
3. Add rice and 2 eggs, coarsely chopped. Season to taste.
4. Shake over heat for a few minutes.
5. Beat egg, cream or milk and mustard together. Stir into kipper mixture in pan.
6. When hot, arrange in a serving dish and keep hot.
7. Grill remaining kipper fillets. Place on top of kedgeree.
8. Garnish with quarters of hard-boiled egg and sprigs of parsley.

ABERDEEN EGGS
Serves 4

1 packet frozen kipper fillets, thawed
1½oz (37gm) flour
scant ½ pint (scant 250ml) milk
salt and pepper
1 tablespoon lemon juice
4 hard-boiled eggs
1 egg, beaten with 1 tablespoon water
4 tablespoons breadcrumbs
fat or oil for deep frying

1. Poach kipper fillets in a little water for 5 minutes. Drain, cool, skin and flake the fish.
2. Melt butter in a pan, stir in flour off the heat and blend in milk.
3. Return to heat and bring to boil, stirring continuously.
4. Season and add fish and lemon juice. Beat mixture well and leave to cool.
5. Divide into four and coat each egg with the mixture. Shape by rolling on a floured board.
6. Dip in beaten egg and coat with crumbs.
7. Chill thoroughly before frying in hot, deep fat, for 4–5 minutes, or until g lden brown. Drain and serve.

KIPPER AND EGG FILLED BAKED POTATOES
Serves 4

4 large potatoes
1 packet frozen kipper fillets, thawed
4 hard-boiled eggs, chopped
4oz (100gm) Cheddar cheese, grated
4 teaspoons prepared mustard
4oz (100gm) butter, melted
2 tablespoons milk
salt and pepper

1. Preheat oven to moderate, 350 deg F or gas 4 (180 deg C).
2. Wash potatoes and prick with a fork.
3. Bake in centre of oven for 1 hour.
4. Increase oven setting to hot, 425 deg F or gas 7 (220 deg C).
5. Cut kippers into ½-inch pieces and combine with chopped egg and half the grated cheese in a large mixing bowl.
6. Cut baked potatoes in half lengthways, scoop out centre and add to kipper mixture.
7. Add mustard, butter and milk, and stir thoroughly. Season to taste.
8. Place potato shells on a baking tray and fill generously with mixture.
9. Sprinkle tops with remaining cheese and bake in centre of oven for 15–20 minutes, or until golden brown.

BRAZILIAN FISH ROLLS
Serves 4

2 bananas
juice of 1 lemon
1 large packet frozen whole plaice, thawed
2oz (50gm) flour, seasoned with salt and pepper
1 egg, beaten
3oz (75gm) fresh breadcrumbs
fat for deep frying
lemon wedges to garnish

1. Peel bananas, cut in half lengthways and sprinkle with lemon juice.
2. Skin fish fillets and sprinkle with lemon juice.
3. Wrap each fillet around a halved banana, securing with a toothpick.
4. Dip in seasoned flour and coat with egg and crumbs.
5. Fry in deep fat for 4 minutes until golden brown. Drain.
6. Serve at once, garnished with lemon wedges.

SUPPER CROUSTADES
Serves 4

4 firm, round, bread rolls
2oz (50gm) butter, melted
1oz (25gm) flour
¼ pint (125ml) fresh single cream
2 tablespoons lemon juice
grated rind of half a lemon
6oz (150gm) smoked haddock, cooked and flaked
8oz (200gm) cottage cheese
1 tablespoon chopped chives
1 tablespoon chopped parsley
salt and pepper

1. Preheat oven to moderately hot, 400 deg F or gas 6 (200 deg C).
2. Cut the top off each roll and scoop out the soft centres.
3. Brush insides and lid with melted butter.
4. Place on baking tin in centre of oven for 10 minutes.
5. Mix flour with rest of melted butter in a saucepan and allow to cook for 1 minute without browning. Remove from heat and slowly blend in cream.
6. Bring to the boil, stirring well.
7. Reduce heat, stir in lemon juice and grated rind, haddock, cottage cheese and herbs.
8. Season to taste. Heat mixture through, spoon into rolls and top with a 'lid'.

SAVOURY FISH TOAST
Serves 4

8oz (200gm) cooked smoked
haddock (Finnan haddock)
1oz (25gm) butter
½oz (12gm) flour
¼ pint (125ml) milk and water
pepper
4 pieces hot, buttered toast

1. Flake fish, removing bones.
2. Melt butter and add flour.
Gradually add liquid, bring to the
boil and cook well.
3. Add fish, season with pepper
and pile mixture on toast.

NORWEGIAN FISH SUPPER
Serves 4

1lb (½ kilo) cooked potatoes
1lb (½ kilo) boiled white fish,
flaked
¾ pint (375ml) white sauce (see
Basic recipes, page 100)
salt and pepper
a little grated nutmeg

1. Chop the potatoes, then cook
them with fish in white sauce for
a few minutes.
2. Season well with salt, pepper
and nutmeg.
3. Serve hot, dredged with more
nutmeg.

MUSHROOM AND HERRING ROE SAVOURY
Serves 4

1 can (8oz or 200gm) soft
herring roes
1oz (25gm) flour
1oz (25gm) butter
2oz (50gm) button mushrooms
1 tablespoon flour
½ pint (250ml) milk
salt and pepper
juice and zest of half a lemon
4 slices hot, buttered toast
lemon twists and sprigs of
parsley to garnish

1. Drain roes, dust with flour and
fry in butter until golden brown.
Remove and keep warm.
2. Cook mushrooms in butter in
same pan, then remove.
3. Add flour to pan and allow to
cook gently.
4. Gradually add milk, stirring
continuously until thickened.
5. Return mushrooms to pan and
add salt, pepper and lemon juice
and zest.
6. Arrange roes on hot, buttered
toast, pour sauce over and serve
garnished with lemon twists and
parsley.

DEVILLED ROES ON TOAST
Serves 4

2oz (50gm) flour
1 large can herring roes
1 small onion
2oz (50gm) butter
1½ teaspoons curry powder
2 teaspoons chutney
salt and pepper
4 rounds buttered toast, crusts
removed

1. Flour the roes.
2. Skin and chop the onion and
cook it in butter, then add roes
and cook quickly to brown them
on both sides.
3. Remove roes from pan.
4. Add the curry powder, chutney,
salt and pepper to pan.
5. Cook, mixing well, then return
the herring roes to the pan.
6. Serve the mixture piping hot
on hot, buttered toast.

HERRING ROE BOUCHEES
Serves 4

1oz (25gm) butter
4oz (100gm) button mushrooms,
chopped
juice of 1 lemon
1 can soft herring roes
½ teaspoon pepper
salt to taste
8 individual bouchée (small vol
au vent) cases
sprigs of parsley to garnish

1. Melt butter in a saucepan, add
mushrooms and lemon juice, and
cover with a lid.
2. Cook for 2 minutes, shaking
pan occasionally.
3. Add soft herring roes and
continue cooking for 2–3 minutes,
stirring continuously.
4. Season with pepper and, if
liked, extra salt.
5. Spoon mixture into hot pastry
cases and garnish with sprigs of
parsley. Serve immediately or
chill and serve cold with salad.

CURRIED HERRINGS
Serves 4

4 herrings
2oz (50gm) butter
2 small teaspoons curry paste
½ teaspoon curry powder
a squeeze of lemon juice

1. Clean and fillet the herrings.
2. Cream butter and work in
curry paste, curry powder and
lemon juice.
3. Spread over the fish and grill.
4. Serve at once on a hot dish,
garnished with lemon slices.

BUCKLING PATE
Serves 4–6

This is a favourite of mine.

1 large buckling
4oz (100gm) butter
1 garlic clove, crushed
1 tablespoon lemon juice
freshly ground black pepper

1. Skin and take the bones out of the buckling.
2. Pound the buckling flesh and butter with a wooden spoon.
3. Add garlic and lemon juice. Season with pepper and press mixture into pots.
4. Serve, spread on toast, with salad.

QUICK PIZZAS
Serves 6

1 onion, finely chopped
1 tablespoon oil
1 small can tomatoes
salt and pepper
½ teaspoon Tabasco sauce
1 small can tuna steak, drained
1 tablespoon tomato purée
6 crumpets
1 can anchovy fillets
black olives
grated Parmesan cheese

1. Fry onion in oil until soft.
2. Add tomatoes, salt and pepper and cook gently for 30 minutes.
3. Remove from heat and add Tabasco sauce, tuna steak and tomato purée.
4. Stir well and spread the mixture equally on to crumpets.
5. Garnish each with a lattice of anchovy fillets, halved black olives, and sprinkle with Parmesan cheese.
6. Grill slowly to heat right through, then serve immediately.

SALMON PUFFS
Makes 18–20 puffs

puff pastry made with 8oz (200gm) flour (see Basic recipes, page 100)
1 large can red salmon
juice of half a lemon
1 small can cream
2 level teaspoons chopped parsley
salt and pepper
1 egg, beaten

1. Preheat oven to hot, 450 deg F or gas 8 (230 deg C).
2. Roll out pastry very thinly and cut it into 4-inch diameter circles.
3. Drain the salmon and mix with all the other ingredients except beaten egg.
4. Put a small teaspoonful of mixture in the centre of the circles and seal together.
5. Flute the edges and glaze with beaten egg.
6. Bake in centre of oven for 10 minutes, then reduce the heat and cook in a moderate oven, 350 deg F or gas 4 (180 deg C) for a further 10 minutes.

SHRIMP AND EGG MORNAY
Serves 4

1 packet cheese sauce mix
½ pint (250ml) milk
4 hard-boiled eggs, chopped
1 can (4oz or 100gm) shrimps
1oz (25gm) butter
1oz (25gm) cheese, grated
2 tablespoons fresh, white breadcrumbs

1. Make up cheese sauce as directed on packet, using milk.
2. Add eggs, shrimps and butter, then pour into scallop shells or individual fireproof dishes.
3. Mix cheese and breadcrumbs together and sprinkle over the mixture.
4. Brown under the grill and serve.

CAPPED MUSHROOMS
Serves 4

8 large mushrooms
1oz (25gm) butter
1oz (25gm) bacon, cooked and chopped
½oz (12gm) breadcrumbs
½oz (12gm) cheese, grated
¼ teaspoon chopped parsley
1 small onion, chopped
salt and pepper
1 egg

1. Preheat oven to moderate to moderately hot, 375 deg F or gas 5 (190 deg C).
2. Remove mushroom stalks and chop them finely.
3. Melt butter and mix in bacon, crumbs and cheese.
4. Add parsley and onion and season well to taste.
5. Bind with beaten egg.
6. Arrange four mushroom caps in a buttered dish.
7. Pile on stuffing and top with the rest of the mushrooms.
8. Bake in centre of oven for 15 minutes.

MUSHROOMS IN CREAM
Serves 4

1lb (½ kilo) large mushrooms
1 small onion
2 bacon rashers
2oz (50gm) butter
salt and pepper
¼ pint (125ml) single cream

1. Preheat oven to moderate to moderately hot, 375 deg F or gas 5 (190 deg C).
2. Chop mushroom stalks, onion and bacon and fry in butter until tender.
3. Season and spoon a little of the mixture on to each mushroom cap.
4. Set them in a casserole and pour cream over.
5. Cover and bake in centre of oven for 30 minutes.

PEPPERS STUFFED WITH MUSHROOM RISOTTO
Serves 4

4 red or green peppers
6oz (150gm) mushrooms, sliced
1 large onion, sliced
3 tablespoons vegetable oil
12oz (300gm) long-grain rice
2 tablespoons single cream
¼ pint (125ml) beef stock
freshly ground black pepper

1. Preheat oven to moderate, 350 deg F or gas 4 (180 deg C).
2. Cut peppers in half lengthways. Pour boiling water over them and leave to stand for 30 minutes.
3. Fry mushrooms and onion in oil until brown.
4. Add rice, cream and stock and let it simmer over a low heat for 5 minutes.
5. Add pepper to taste.
6. Drain peppers and fill with rice mixture.
7. Spoon any remaining risotto into the base of a casserole with the red peppers on top.
8. Cover and bake in centre of oven for 30 minutes. Serve with a salad.

HOT STUFFED TOMATOES
Serves 4

8 even-sized tomatoes
3oz (75gm) ham, chopped
2 teaspoons chopped onion
1oz (25gm) butter
4 tablespoons fresh breadcrumbs
1 teaspoon chopped parsley
salt and pepper
4 rounds of fried bread

1. Preheat oven to moderate, 350 deg F or gas 4 (180 deg C).
2. Wipe the tomatoes and cut a small round from the top of each. Remove the inside with a teaspoon.
3. Fry ham and onion in butter and add crumbs, parsley, seasoning and tomato pulp.
4. Fill the tomatoes with this mixture and replace the lids.
5. Bake in centre of oven for about 15 minutes.
6. Serve on fried bread.

CRISPY STUFFED ROLLS
(Illustrated on page 35)
Serves 2

4 crisp dinner rolls
1oz (25gm) butter
1 small onion
2oz (50gm) mushrooms
3 tomatoes
3 eggs
salt and pepper

1. Preheat oven to moderate, 350 deg F or gas 4 (180 deg C).
2. Cut a round from top of each roll with a small plain pastry cutter or knife. Hollow out to leave a shell.
3. Melt butter, grate onion, chop mushrooms and peel and chop tomatoes.
4. Add vegetables to butter and fry gently for 5–10 minutes or until soft.
5. Beat eggs with seasoning, pour into pan and stir with a wooden spoon over a low heat until mixture thickens.
6. Pile filling into bread shells and replace rounds of bread to form lids.
7. Put on a baking sheet and cook in centre of oven for about 15 minutes, until rolls are crisp and filling heated through.

ONION TOP HATS
(Illustrated on page 35)
Serves 4

2oz (50gm) liver
1 streaky bacon rasher
4 large onions
1oz (25gm) breadcrumbs
1 dessertspoon chopped parsley
½ level teaspoon mixed herbs
grated rind of half a lemon
salt and pepper
2oz (50gm) dripping

1. Preheat oven to moderate to moderately hot, 375 deg F or gas 5 (190 deg C).
2. Chop liver and bacon and mix together.
3. Skin the onions and put them into a pan of boiling water for 10 minutes. Drain and take out the centres.
4. Chop the centres and mix with liver and bacon, breadcrumbs, parsley, mixed herbs and lemon rind. Season well.
5. Mix thoroughly and stuff into the onions.
6. Stand the onions in a casserole dish, add the dripping and cover with foil or a lid.
7. Bake in centre of oven for 1 hour.

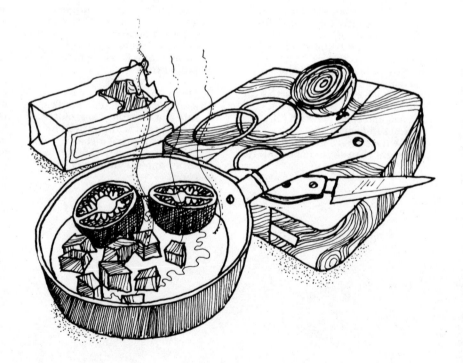

POTATO SURPRISES

(Illustrated on page 18)
Serves 4

Baked potatoes with sausages and cheese hidden inside them.

4 large potatoes
1 teaspoon salt
4 pork sausages
4 streaky bacon rashers
1½oz (37gm) butter
1oz (25gm) cheese, grated
salt and pepper
1 tablespoon cream

1. Preheat oven to moderately hot, 400 deg F or gas 6 (200 deg C).
2. Scrub the potatoes, rub with salt, prick and bake in centre of oven for 45 minutes.
3. Twist the sausages into small pieces. Prick and bake in the oven with the potatoes for 20 minutes.
4. Chop bacon rashers and fry till crisp.
5. Cut potatoes in half lengthways and scoop out most of the centre.
6. Brush with a little melted butter. Add cheese and season well.
7. Fill potatoes with the pieces of sausages and bacon.
8. Serve on a hot dish surrounded with the rest of the potatoes mashed with remaining butter and the cream.
9. Garnish with tomato quarters and sprigs of watercress.

SAVOURY EGG NESTS

Serves 4

1¼lb (¾ kilo) potatoes
1 small onion, grated
1oz (25gm) butter
2 tablespoons milk
salt and pepper
4 eggs

1. Preheat oven to moderate to moderately hot, 375 deg F or gas 5 (190 deg C).
2. Boil potatoes and mash them thoroughly.
3. Add onion, butter, milk and seasoning and beat well.
4. Spoon into four small ovenware dishes and leave a hollow in the centre. Break an egg into each.
5. Bake in centre of oven for 20–25 minutes until eggs are set.

POTATO RAREBITS

Serves 4

4 large potatoes
2oz (50gm) butter
salt and pepper
4oz (100gm) cooked ham, chopped
4 slices cheese

1. Preheat oven to hot, 425 deg F or gas 7 (220 deg C).
2. Scrub the potatoes, dry them, then prick with a fork. Bake in centre of oven for 1–1½ hours or until soft.
3. Cut a slice from the top of each one, scoop out insides, mash with butter, adding seasonings to taste and ham.
4. Refill the shells and put a slice of cheese on top.
5. Place under a hot grill until the cheese bubbles and browns lightly.

POTATO BOATS

Serves 4

4 large potatoes
8 sole or plaice fillets
2oz (50gm) butter
salt and pepper
8 processed cheese slices

1. Preheat oven to hot, 425 deg F or gas 7 (220 deg C).
2. Wash and scrub the potatoes, dry and prick with a fork.
3. Place on the centre shelf of oven for 1–1½ hours, or until tender.
4. Roll up the fillets and top with a little butter.
5. Place the fish in a covered dish on the second shelf down of the oven 15 minutes before potatoes are cooked.
6. When the potatoes are cooked, cut them in half lengthways, scoop out the pulp into a bowl, beat in remaining butter and season to taste.
7. Pile back into the shells and top each one with a fillet of fish, then place a cheese slice on top of each.
8. Put back into the oven until cheese has melted. Serve immediately.

POTATO NESTS

Serves 4

6oz (150gm) mushrooms
1 dessertspoon grated onion
2lb (1 kilo) creamed potatoes
4 eggs
2 tablespoons grated cheese

1. Preheat oven to moderate, 350 deg F or gas 4 (180 deg C).
2. Finely chop the mushrooms and mix with the onion.
3. Add to the potatoes and beat well.
4. Shape into four nest shapes on an ovenware serving dish.
5. Break an egg into each nest and sprinkle with grated cheese.
6. Bake in centre of oven for 20 minutes or until the eggs are set.

ITALIAN ASPARAGUS

Serves 2

1 medium can asparagus spears
2 slices hot toast
8oz (200gm) grated cheese (Parmesan if available)
4oz (100gm) butter, melted

1. Heat asparagus spears gently, drain and place on hot toast on a dish. Sprinkle with grated cheese.
2. Pour melted butter liberally over the top and brown quickly under the grill.

CHEESE AND POTATO BITES

Serves 4

1¼lb (¾ kilo) potatoes
½oz (12gm) butter
½ teaspoon made mustard
3oz (75gm) cheese, grated
salt and pepper
1 egg, beaten
2oz (50gm) breadcrumbs
fat for frying

1. Peel and boil the potatoes. Sieve when tender and mash while still hot.
2. Add butter, mustard, cheese, seasoning and sufficient egg to bind.
3. Shape into bite-sized balls, brush with egg and roll in breadcrumbs.
4. Fry in hot fat until golden brown; drain and serve with salad.

CHEESE D'ARTOIS
Serves 4

puff pastry made with 4oz
(100gm) flour (see Basic
recipes, page 100)
1 egg
2oz (50gm) Parmesan cheese
salt and pepper
pinch of cayenne pepper
1oz (25gm) butter
watercress

1. Preheat oven to hot, 450 deg F
or gas 8 (230 deg C).
2. Roll the pastry thinly and
divide equally into two.
3. Beat the egg and add to the
grated cheese, salt, pepper and
cayenne.
4. Add the melted butter.
5. Spread this mixture on one
half of the pastry, wet the edges
and place the other half over it.
6. Press the edges together, brush
the top with a little beaten egg
and mark across in fingers.
7. Bake on second shelf of oven
for about 15 minutes, until golden
brown on top and underneath,
then divide where the pastry is
marked.
8. Serve hot or cold, garnished
with watercress.

CHEESE AND RICE BALLS
Serves 4–8

1 egg, lightly beaten
1 tablespoon horseradish
cream or relish
½ teaspoon salt
½ teaspoon dry mustard
1 teaspoon Worcestershire
sauce
¼ teaspoon pepper
8oz (200gm) boiled long-grain
rice (raw weight)
3oz (75gm) Cheddar cheese,
grated
4oz (100gm) rice krispies, finely
crushed

1. Combine egg, horseradish, salt,
mustard, Worcestershire sauce
and pepper in a mixing bowl.
2. Add rice and cheese and mix
thoroughly. Chill.
3. Roll mixture into small balls
about ¾ inch in diameter.
4. Roll in crushed rice krispies.
5. Fry in deep hot fat (375 deg F
or 190 deg C) for about 3 minutes
until golden brown.
6. Drain on absorbent paper, then
serve piping hot on sticks.

CHEESE AND MUSHROOM TURNOVERS
Serves 4–6

shortcrust pastry made with
8oz (200gm) flour (see Basic
recipes, page 100)
½oz (12gm) butter
4oz (100gm) mushrooms, sliced
4oz (100gm) Cheddar cheese,
cut into small cubes
salt and pepper
pinch of cayenne pepper
little milk

1. Preheat oven to moderately
hot, 400 deg F or gas 6 (200 deg C).
2. Roll pastry out to ⅛ inch thick
and cut into six large circles.
3. Melt butter in a frying pan and
gently fry mushrooms.
4. Drain mushrooms and add
them to cheese. Season well.
5. Divide mushroom and cheese
mixture among the six rounds of
pastry, brush edges with milk,
fold pastry over and seal edges
together.
6. Brush the turnovers with milk,
place on a greased baking sheet
and bake in centre of oven for
25–30 minutes.

COTTAGE CHEESE COCOTTES
Serves 4

2oz (50gm) butter, melted
8oz (200gm) cottage cheese
2 eggs
1 small onion
1 slice cooked ham
4oz (100gm) button mushrooms
salt and pepper
1 tablespoon freshly chopped
parsley, chervil or tarragon

1. Preheat oven to moderately
hot, 400 deg F or gas 6 (200 deg C).
2. Brush four individual ovenware
dishes with half the butter and
arrange on a baking sheet.
3. Beat cottage cheese and eggs
together.
4. Chop the onion and cook
gently until tender but not brown,
in rest of butter.
5. Chop and stir ham,
mushrooms and onion into
cheese and egg mixture. Season
to taste.
6. Mix in fresh herbs, divide
mixture into the four dishes and
cook in centre of oven for 10–15
minutes.

GOLDEN PUFFS
Serves 4

1½lb (¾ kilo) boiled potatoes
½oz (12gm) butter
½ teaspoon made mustard
3oz (75gm) Cheddar cheese,
grated
salt and pepper
1 egg, beaten
2oz (50gm) breadcrumbs
fat for frying
4 pork sausages

1. Heat potatoes in a pan and
mash them thoroughly with
butter.
2. Add mustard, cheese, salt and
pepper and sufficient egg to bind.
3. Shape into balls and roll in
crumbs.
4. Deep fry until golden brown,
then drain on absorbent paper.
5. Fry the sausages and cut into
pieces, then spike pieces on to a
cocktail stick with a golden puff.

CHEESE AND POTATO FLAN
Serves 4

shortcrust pastry made with
6oz (150gm) flour (see Basic
recipes, page 100)
1 large potato, peeled and
finely grated
2oz (50gm) cheese, grated
2 eggs, beaten
salt and pepper
¼ pint (125ml) single cream or
rich milk
chopped chives

1. Preheat oven to moderately
hot, 400 deg F or gas 6 (200 deg C).
2. Use pastry to line an 8-inch
(20cm) flan ring, prick all over
and bake blind in centre of oven
for about 20 minutes. (Do not
allow to brown too much.)
3. Mix together potatoes, cheese,
eggs, salt, pepper and cream or
milk.
4. Pour into flan case and sprinkle
with chopped chives.
5. Return to oven and bake for a
further 30–35 minutes. Serve hot
cut in slices.

Kebabs alfresco with baked beans (see page 21)

Crispy stuffed rolls (see page 32)

Hot sausages and cheese dip (see page 23)

Onion top hats (see page 32)

Chicken casserole (see page 45)   Steak cobbler (see page 38)

Cheese squares (see page 52)   Hunter's veal (see page 40)

CHEESE PANCAKES
Serves 4

4oz (100gm) self-raising flour
pinch of salt
1 packet cheese sauce mix
2 eggs, beaten
½ pint (250ml) milk
corn oil for frying
1 small onion, finely sliced
1oz (25gm) butter
3 small tomatoes, peeled and
chopped
2–4oz (50–100gm) small
mushrooms, sliced

1. Sieve flour and salt together.
2. Stir in contents of packet of
cheese sauce.
3. Stir in eggs and milk and beat
well.
4. Heat a little corn oil in a small
frying pan and make small
pancakes, using all the mixture.
Keep hot.
5. To make the filling, fry onion
in butter, add tomatoes and
mushrooms and cook until tender.
6. Spread some filling on each
pancake and roll up. Serve hot.

GRILLED APPLE SNACKS
Serves 4

4oz (100gm) cream cheese
4 slices hot toast
2 large apples
1 tablespoon brown sugar
4 bacon rashers

1. Spread cream cheese on the
slices of toast. Keep hot.
2. Peel apples, remove cores, then
grate and cover the slices of toast
with the apple. Sprinkle with
sugar.
3. Cut bacon rashers in half and
remove rinds.
4. Put pieces of bacon on each
apple snack.
5. Put under the grill and brown
for 3 minutes.

BACON CHEESE FINGERS
Serves 4

1 packet scone mix
shake of paprika
6oz (150gm) cheese, finely
grated
3oz (75gm) bacon trimmings,
chopped
¼ pint (125ml) milk
1 egg, beaten

1. Preheat oven to hot, 425 deg F
or gas 7 (220 deg C).
2. Mix scone mix with paprika,
5oz (125gm) cheese and bacon.
3. Mix with milk and most of the
egg to give a soft dough.
4. Divide into 12 pieces and roll
into fingers, brush with remaining
beaten egg and roll in remaining
cheese.
5. Put on a greased baking tin
and bake in centre of oven for
20–25 minutes.

TOASTED CHEESE SLICES WITH ASPARAGUS
Serves 4

1oz (25gm) butter
6oz (150gm) cheese, grated
3 tablespoons milk
few drops Worcestershire
sauce
pinch of cayenne pepper
salt
4 slices toast
butter to spread
1 medium can asparagus

1. Melt butter and cheese over a
very gentle heat.
2. Add milk gradually as the
cheese melts, and season with
Worcestershire sauce, cayenne
pepper and salt.
3. Cook gently until sauce
thickens and is smooth and
creamy.
4. Put toast on grill rack and
spread generously with butter.
5. Lay drained asparagus on
toast and coat with cheese sauce.
6. Grill until lightly browned
and serve at once.

CHEESE FLUFFS
Serves 4

2oz (50gm) cheese
2oz (50gm) small mushrooms
deep fat for frying
2 egg whites
salt and pepper
watercress to garnish

1. Grate cheese and halve the
mushrooms. Fry mushrooms in a
little hot fat. Drain and keep hot.
2. Whisk egg whites until stiff,
then add salt and pepper
3. Fold in half the cheese and
drop the mixture in teaspoonfuls
into the hot fat. Cook until
golden brown, then drain well.
4. Pile into a hot dish with the
mushrooms.
5. Serve piping hot sprinkled with
rest of cheese and garnished with
watercress.

INDIVIDUAL SPINACH AND GREEN PEPPER QUICHES
Serves 4

shortcrust pastry made with
4oz (100gm) flour (see Basic
recipes, page 100)
1oz (25gm) butter
1 medium onion, finely chopped
1 small green pepper, finely
chopped
1 egg
¼ pint (125ml) single cream
1 packet (8oz or 200gm) frozen
spinach, thawed
salt and pepper
¼ teaspoon nutmeg

1. Preheat oven to moderately hot,
400 deg F or gas 6 (200 deg C).
2. Roll pastry out and line four
4-inch (10cm) tartlet tins.
3. Bake blind in centre of oven
for 10 minutes.
4. Remove from oven and reduce
oven temperature to moderate,
350 deg F or gas 4 (180 deg C).
5. Meanwhile, melt butter in a
pan and cook onion and green
pepper together until soft but not
coloured.
6. Beat together egg and cream
and stir in spinach, cooked onion
and green pepper.
7. Season to taste with salt,
pepper and nutmeg.
8. Fill the tartlet cases with this
mixture and return to oven for 20
minutes or until firm.

Family sit-down suppers

Here is a selection of nourishing recipes that is bound to please every member of your family, whatever their particular favourites happen to be.

CASSEROLE OF BEEF
Serves 4

1lb ($\frac{1}{2}$ kilo) chuck steak or leg beef
2oz (50gm) flour, seasoned with salt and pepper
1oz (25gm) fat
1 onion
2 carrots
1 leek
2 sticks celery
small piece turnip
$\frac{1}{2}$ level teaspoon salt
$\frac{1}{2}$ level teaspoon pepper
1 teaspoon tomato purée
$\frac{3}{4}$ pint (375ml) beef stock

1. Wipe the meat and remove any fat. Cut it up, roll in seasoned flour and fry in fat.
2. Prepare the vegetables, cut into small pieces and add to meat. Fry gently for 5 minutes.
3. Add seasoning and tomato purée.
4. Stir in the stock and bring up to simmering point.
5. Cover with lid and cook gently for 2 hours.
6. Garnish with carrots and peas and serve with new potatoes.

STEAK COBBLER
(Illustrated on page 36)
Serves 4

1 large can stewed steak
1 large packet frozen, mixed vegetables, thawed
1 packet scone mix
4oz (100gm) cheese, grated

1. Preheat oven to moderate to moderately hot, 375 deg F or gas 5 (190 deg C).
2. Mix steak and vegetables in an ovenware dish.
3. Make up scone mix as directed on packet and add cheese.
4. Pat out flat and cut into 10 rounds with a pastry cutter.
5. Arrange on top of dish and cook on second shelf down of oven for 30 minutes.

ITALIAN RICE PIZZA
Serves 4–6

4oz (100gm) boiled long-grain rice (raw weight)
2 eggs, beaten
6oz (150gm) cheese, grated
3oz (75gm) onion, finely chopped
1 tablespoon vegetable oil
$\frac{1}{2}$ pint (250ml) tomato sauce
1 garlic clove, crushed
8oz (200gm) minced beef
$\frac{1}{2}$ teaspoon salt
pepper
6 stuffed olives, sliced
1 small can mushrooms, sliced

1. Preheat oven to hot, 450 deg F or gas 8 (230 deg C).
2. Mix rice with eggs and 4oz (100gm) cheese. Press in a greased 12-inch (30cm) pizza pan or pie dish and bake in centre of oven for 15 minutes.
3. Fry onion in oil until tender.
4. Add tomato sauce and garlic and simmer for 20 minutes.
5. Mix in beef and salt and pepper to taste.
6. Spread this mixture to within 1 inch of edge of baked rice crust.
7. Top with remaining cheese, the olives and mushrooms.
8. Bake in centre of oven for about 10 minutes, or until cheese is melted and sauce hot.

CHEESE-TOPPED MEAT CAKE
Serves 6

3 tablespoons olive oil
4 streaky bacon rashers
1 onion
1 leek
1lb (½ kilo) lean beef, minced
¼ teaspoon basil
¼ teaspoon parsley
¼ teaspoon coriander
1 teaspoon ground mace
¼ teaspoon allspice
1 garlic clove, crushed
1 tablespoon wine vinegar
1 small can tomato purée
1 large aubergine or 2 tomatoes
8oz (200gm) potatoes
½oz (12gm) butter
½oz (12gm) flour
¼ pint (125ml) milk
1 egg
1oz (25gm) cheese, grated
salt and pepper

1. Preheat oven to very moderate, 325 deg F or gas 3 (170 deg C).
2. Heat 1 tablespoon oil in a large heavy pan.
3. Chop bacon, onion and leek and add to the pan.
4. Cook until all the vegetables are tender but not browned.
5. Add minced beef, basil, parsley, coriander, mace, allspice and garlic, and cook until lightly browned.
6. Add wine vinegar and tomato purée and simmer gently for 15 minutes.
7. Cut aubergine or tomatoes into ¼-inch slices. Sprinkle with salt and leave for 10 minutes; if using aubergine, drain and rinse well.
8. Wipe aubergine slices with a dry cloth and fry in remaining oil in a pan.
9. Cover the bottom of a greased 2½-pint (approximately 1¼ litre) casserole with some aubergine or tomato slices.
10. Transfer the simmering beef to the casserole.
11. Cover with remaining aubergine or tomato slices and thinly sliced potatoes.
12. Melt butter in a pan, add flour and cook for 1 minute.
13. Beat in the milk and cook until thickened.
14. Remove from heat and stir in egg and cheese.
15. Season well and pour over the potatoes.
16. Cover casserole and cook in centre of oven for 1 hour.

MUTTON AND MUSHROOMS
Serves 4

4 lamb cutlets
salt and pepper
3 tablespoons cream
8oz (200gm) mushrooms
½oz (12gm) butter
3 tomatoes
1 teaspoon chopped parsley

1. Preheat oven to very moderate, 325 deg F or gas 3 (170 deg C).
2. Put cutlets into a buttered pie dish and season well.
3. Spoon cream and mushrooms over.
4. Dot with butter and cover with foil or a well fitting lid.
5. Bake in centre of oven for 1¼ hours.
6. After 45 minutes baking, slice the tomatoes on the top, replace lid and continue cooking.
7. Sprinkle with parsley to serve.

LAYERED LAMB CASSEROLE
Serves 4

4 fat streaky bacon rashers, rinded
1½lb (¾ kilo) white spring cabbage
8 cutlets middle or best end neck of lamb
salt and pepper
1 teaspoon caraway seeds
4 tablespoons water
1lb (½ kilo) potatoes, peeled and sliced

1. Preheat oven to moderate, 350 deg F or gas 4 (180 deg C).
2. Put bacon in a large casserole.
3. Slice cabbage finely and fill casserole with layers of cabbage and lamb.
4. Sprinkle seasoning and caraway seeds on each layer.
5. Pour in water, top with a layer of potatoes and cover casserole.
6. Cook in centre of oven for 1½ hours.
7. Remove lid and add a little more water, then cook uncovered for a further 20 minutes to brown crust.

HOTPOT WITH BEANS
Serves 4–6

Here is a version of the Lancashire hot pot which includes runner beans.

2lb (1 kilo) scrag end neck of lamb
2½lb (1¼ kilo) potatoes
8oz (200gm) onions, skinned
4oz (100gm) mushrooms
1 pint (approximately ½ litre) stock
salt and pepper
8oz (200gm) runner beans, sliced

1. Trim and cut up meat and turn it into a pan.
2. Peel and slice the potatoes and onions.
3. Add to the pan with the halved mushrooms.
3. Pour in the stock, season and simmer in a covered pan for 1½ hours.
4. Add beans and more stock if required and simmer for a further 15 minutes.

LAMB AND APPLE PIE
Serves 4

Lamb chops and apples make a surprisingly good mixture when baked together in a pie.

shortcrust pastry made with 6oz (150gm) flour (see Basic recipes, page 100)
1½lb (¾ kilo) cooking apples
4 chump chops
salt and pepper
2 onions
½ pint (250ml) water

1. Preheat oven to hot, 425 deg F or gas 7 (220 deg C).
2. Roll out pastry and line a 2-pint (approximately 1 litre) pie dish, leaving enough pastry for the top of pie.
3. Peel and slice the apples.
4. Turn apples and chops into the pie dish, season and add sliced onion.
5. Pour ½ pint (250ml) water over.
6. Cover with pastry top and bake in centre of oven for 10 minutes, then for a further 45 minutes at moderate to moderately hot, 375 deg F or gas 5 (190 deg C).

PEPPERED LAMB CASSEROLE
Serves 6

3lb (1½ kilo) shoulder of lamb
1 teaspoon salt
½ teaspoon black pepper
good pinch of cayenne
1 teaspoon ground mace
4 tablespoons oil
1 onion, chopped
1 garlic clove
¼ pint (125ml) red wine
3 peppers, shredded (red and green mixed)
1½lb (¾ kilo) tomatoes, skinned and sliced
1 level tablespoon chopped parsley

1. Bone the lamb and cut the meat into 2-inch squares, removing any excess fat from the meat.
2. Turn into a bowl and sprinkle with half the salt, black pepper, cayenne pepper and mace. Leave for 30 minutes then turn meat over and sprinkle with rest of seasoning.
3. Meanwhile, preheat oven to moderate, 350 deg F or gas 4 (180 deg C).
4. Fry meat in oil until golden, then add onion and crushed garlic and cook until tender.
5. Heat wine in a separate pan and when hot ignite with a match, then let the flames die down. Pour over meat.
6. Turn into a casserole, blanch shredded peppers in boiling water for 2 minutes and add to casserole.
7. Cook on bottom shelf of oven for 1½ hours.
8. Add tomatoes 20 minutes before the end of cooking time.
9. Sprinkle with parsley and serve with boiled rice and courgettes.

PORK CHOPS IN APPLE SAUCE
Serves 4

4 pork chops
1½oz (37gm) lard
1½lb (¾ kilo) cooking apples
juice of 1 lemon
1oz (25gm) brown sugar
1oz (25gm) butter

1. Preheat oven to moderate to moderately hot, 375 deg F or gas 5 (190 deg C).
2. Fry pork chops in lard.
3. Peel and core apples and slice thinly; place in a pan.
4. Add lemon juice and sugar.
5. Add butter and leave to simmer until reduced to a pulp.
6. Put chops into a casserole and pour apple sauce over. Cover and bake in centre of oven for 1 hour.

HUNTER'S VEAL
(Illustrated on page 36)
Serves 4

4 thin slices of veal
salt and pepper
2oz (50gm) butter
1 onion, finely chopped
1 garlic clove, crushed
2oz (50gm) mushroom stalks, chopped
1–2 tablespoons white wine or cooking sherry
¼ pint (125ml) brown gravy
1 good tablespoon tomato purée

1. Season veal, melt butter in a frying pan and cook meat quickly on both sides.
2. Remove from pan and fry onion, garlic and mushroom stalks until tender.
3. Add wine or sherry, gravy and tomato purée.
4. Replace meat and simmer gently for about 10 minutes.
5. Serve with boiled spaghetti.

SKEWERED VEAL IN A CASSEROLE
Serves 4

1½lb (¾ kilo) shoulder of veal, boned
1 egg, beaten
2 tablespoons milk
2oz (50gm) breadcrumbs
½ level teaspoon salt
2 level teaspoons mustard
good shake of pepper
1 teaspoon chopped parsley
2oz (50gm) butter
4oz (100gm) boiled long-grain rice (raw weight)
2 tomatoes

1. Preheat oven to 350 deg F or gas 4 (180 deg C).
2. Cut the veal into 2-inch cubes and dip in egg and milk.
3. Mix breadcrumbs with salt, mustard, pepper and parsley.
4. Roll veal in the breadcrumb mixture and brown in hot butter.
5. Thread on to four skewers, pile rice into a casserole and top with skewered veal.
6. Add sliced tomatoes, cover with a piece of greaseproof paper and a lid, and bake on centre shelf of oven for 1 hour.

BAKED VEAL
Serves 4

12oz (300gm) pie veal
4oz (100gm) suet
3oz (75gm) breadcrumbs
salt and pepper
2 eggs
a little gravy to mix
¼ pint (125ml) stock

1. Preheat oven to moderate to moderately hot, 375 deg F or gas 5 (190 deg C).
2. Mince or finely chop the veal and suet.
3. Mix with breadcrumbs and seasoning.
4. Blend in 1 egg and just enough gravy to moisten the mixture.
5. Turn into a pie dish and bake in centre of oven for 1 hour.
6. Beat remaining egg with stock, season and pour over the meat mixture.
7. Return to the oven for a further 15 minutes, or until set.

VEAL AND APPLE PIE
Serves 4

1oz (25gm) butter
salt and pepper
4 veal cutlets
1½lb (¾ kilo) apples
½ lemon
1oz (25gm) sugar
2 tablespoons breadcrumbs
3oz (75gm) cheese, grated

1. Preheat oven to moderate to moderately hot, 375 deg F or gas 5 (190 deg C).
2. Heat butter in a pan and season the cutlets.
3. Cook quickly on both sides in the hot butter.
4. Peel, core and slice the apples. Put into a pan with 1 teaspoon lemon juice, a strip of lemon rind and sugar. Cook until quite tender.
5. Sieve and spread half the apple in the bottom of an ovenware dish.
6. Place cutlets on top and cover with remaining apple.
7. Mix crumbs and cheese together and spread on top. Bake in centre of oven for about 30 minutes.

VEAL WITH CREAM SAUCE
Serves 4

4 pieces of veal, 1-inch thick
2oz (50gm) butter
8oz (200gm) mushrooms, sliced
juice of 1 lemon
½ pint (250ml) fresh cream
¼ pint (125ml) white wine
salt and pepper

1. Fry veal slowly in butter until almost cooked.
2. Add mushrooms and lemon juice and continue cooking until mushrooms are tender.
3. Add cream and bring to the boil.
4. Add white wine and seasoning and continue cooking until sauce has reduced to a rich, creamy consistency.
5. Serve with jacket potatoes.

VEAL AND BACON HOTPOT
Serves 4

1lb (½ kilo) stewing veal, cut into 1½-inch cubes
1½oz (37gm) flour, seasoned with salt and pepper
1 small onion, chopped
8oz (200gm) tomatoes, skinned and sliced
6oz (150gm) streaky bacon, cut into pieces
salt and pepper
¼ pint (125ml) stock
1lb (½ kilo) potatoes, finely sliced

1. Preheat oven to moderate to moderately hot, 375 deg F or gas 5 (190 deg C).
2. Coat veal in seasoned flour.
3. Arrange alternate layers of veal, onion, tomatoes and bacon in a large casserole, seasoning well between each layer.
4. Pour stock over and cover completely with potato.
5. Cover and bake in centre of oven for 1½ hours. Remove lid for the last 30 minutes to brown the potato.

MONDAY SUPPER PLATTER
Serves 4

A delicious way to utilise yesterday's roast beef.

12oz (300gm) cooked cold beef
8oz (200gm) cooked potato
2 small cooked beetroots
1 small onion
1½oz (37gm) butter
3 tablespoons milk
1 teaspoon Worcestershire sauce
salt and pepper

1. Mince beef and potatoes.
2. Shred the peeled beetroots and skin and finely chop onion.
3. Mix all together.
4. Heat butter in a frying pan and add beef mixture.
5. Mix in milk, Worcestershire sauce, salt and pepper.
6. Stir over heat until well heated through. Leave for a while until browned and crisp.
7. Fold in half, omelette-fashion, and serve on a hot dish.

QUICK ITALIAN PANCAKES
Serves 4

½ pint (250ml) pancake batter
(see Basic recipes, page 100)
1 small can bolognaise sauce
4oz (100gm) cooked meat,
minced
2oz (50gm) petite Gruyère
cheese, sieved
parsley sprigs to garnish

1. Make eight pancakes by
pouring a little batter into a small
pan and cooking until brown on
both sides.
2. Keep pancakes hot by piling
them up with greaseproof paper
between each layer.
3. Heat the sauce in a pan with
the minced meat.
4. Fill each pancake with a
spoonful of the mixture and roll
up.
5. Serve on a hot dish with the
rest of the sauce poured over the
top.
6. Sprinkle with cheese, garnish
with parsley and serve at once.

BAKED SAVOURY LIVER
Serves 4

4 slices liver
2oz (50gm) breadcrumbs
1 tablespoon chopped parsley
1oz (25gm) shredded suet
salt and pepper
1 egg yolk
a little milk
4 bacon rashers
4oz (100gm) mushrooms
½ pint (250ml) stock

1. Preheat oven to moderately
hot, 400 deg F or gas 6 (200 deg C).
2. Put liver into a casserole.
3. Mix together breadcrumbs,
parsley, suet, seasoning and egg
yolk.
4. Bind with a little milk and
spread over the liver.
5. Chop up bacon and mushrooms
and scatter over the breadcrumb
mixture.
6. Add stock, cover with a lid and
bake in centre of oven for 1 hour.

LIVER BRAISED IN WINE WITH RICE
Serves 4

1oz (25gm) chicken fat or
margarine
1 tablespoon grated onion
8oz (200gm) liver
1 tablespoon flour, seasoned
with salt and pepper
8oz (200gm) mushrooms
¼ pint (125ml) red wine
4oz (100gm) boiled long-grain
rice (raw weight)
parsley and paprika to garnish

1. Preheat oven to very moderate,
325 deg F or gas 3 (170 deg C).
2. Melt fat and cook onion gently
until soft.
3. Cut liver into pieces, dip in
seasoned flour and fry gently
with onion.
4. Wash and slice mushrooms,
add to liver and cook a few
minutes.
5. Add wine, bring to the boil and
remove to a casserole.
6. Cover tightly and cook in
centre of oven for 45 minutes.
7. Press cooked rice into a ring
tin, press down tightly then turn
on to a dish and pour liver and
mushrooms into centre.
8. Garnish with parsley and
paprika.

OXTAIL SUPPER DISH
Serves 4–6

1 large oxtail
1oz (25gm) flour, seasoned with
salt and pepper
1oz (25gm) dripping
2 or 3 onions
8oz (200gm) haricot beans,
soaked overnight
3 carrots, sliced
1 small bayleaf

1. Cut oxtail into fair-sized pieces
and roll in seasoned flour.
2. Melt dripping in a large
saucepan and cook onion and
oxtail in it for a few minutes.
3. Add the drained beans, carrot
and bayleaf and cover with hot
water. Bring to the boil and
remove any scum.
4. Simmer gently for 3–4 hours
until the meat is quite tender.
5. Leave in the pan to get quite
cold and skim all the fat from the
surface. Reheat.
6. Serve hot with mashed turnips
and creamed potatoes.

LAMB'S KIDNEYS IN YOGURT SAUCE
Serves 4

8 lamb's kidneys
¼ pint (125ml) beef stock
4oz (100gm) mushrooms, sliced
1 tablespoon tomato purée
2 teaspoons prepared English mustard
1 carton (5oz or 125gm) natural yogurt
salt and pepper
1 tablespoon freshly chopped parsley

1. Cover kidneys with boiling water and leave to soak for 30 minutes.
2. Skin kidneys, cut in half and remove core.
3. Place in a saucepan with stock, mushrooms and tomato purée. Cover and cook for 20 minutes or until tender.
4. Stir in mustard and yogurt. Season to taste.
5. Sprinkle with parsley and serve with a tomato and onion salad.

CHINESE PORK SAUSAGES
Serves 4

1lb (½ kilo) pork sausages
½oz (12gm) fat
1 can pineapple pieces
½oz (12gm) cornflour
1 teaspoon dry mustard
2 tablespoons brown sugar
2 teaspoons soy sauce
2 teaspoons Worcestershire sauce
2 tablespoons wine vinegar
¼ cucumber, cut into thin strips
salt and pepper

1. Gently fry the sausages in fat, in a pan.
2. Put them into a serving dish and keep warm.
3. Strain off the juice from the pineapple and make it up to ½ pint (250ml) with water.
4. Pour into a pan and bring to the boil.
5. Blend cornflour, mustard, sugar, soy sauce, Worcestershire sauce and vinegar together in a basin.
6. Add to pineapple juice, stirring all the time. Bring to the boil, still stirring.
7. Add pineapple pieces and strips of cucumber. Season and pour over sausages.

SAUSAGES ESPAGNOLE
Serves 4

8oz (200gm) onions
4 large tomatoes, skinned and sliced
1 rounded tablespoon capers
salt and pepper
1lb (½ kilo) pork sausages

1. Preheat oven to moderate to moderately hot, 375 deg F or gas 5 (190 deg C).
2. Thinly slice the onions and put into a shallow 1½-pint (approximately ¾ litre) casserole.
3. Cover with tomatoes and capers and season with salt and pepper.
4. Arrange the sausages on top.
5. Cover with a lid or piece of aluminium foil and bake in centre of oven for 30–40 minutes.
6. Remove the cover and bake for a further 10–15 minutes until sausages are browned.

SAUSAGE AND POTATO HASH
Serves 4

1lb (½ kilo) potatoes
salt
1oz (25gm) butter
1lb (½ kilo) sausages, sliced
1 onion, thinly sliced
3 tablespoons tomato ketchup
1 teaspoon Worcestershire sauce

1. Parboil potatoes in salted water for about 5 minutes.
2. Strain off the water and let the potatoes dry over the heat. Cut into thick slices.
3. Melt butter in a frying pan, add sausages, onion and potatoes.
4. Cook until lightly browned, turning occasionally.
5. Add tomato ketchup, Worcestershire sauce and salt. Mix thoroughly and serve hot.

SAUSAGE SURPRISE
Serves 4

1lb (½ kilo) pork sausages
1 packet instant potato powder
1 medium onion, chopped
2 bacon rashers, chopped
1 can condensed vegetable soup
5 tablespoons water
cayenne pepper
1oz (25gm) butter

1. Fry the sausages and while they are cooking, make up the instant potato, following instructions on packet.
2. Keep the potatoes warm.
3. When sausages are cooked, remove from pan and keep hot.
4. Pour off excess fat and fry onion and bacon until onion is brown and bacon crisp.
5. Place sausages, bacon and onion in a fireproof dish.
6. Quickly heat soup with water and pour over the sausages.
7. Carefully spoon or pipe the potato over the sausage mixture.
8. Sprinkle with cayenne pepper and dot well with butter.
9. Put under a hot grill for a few minutes, until browned.

STUFFED SAUSAGE ROLL
Serves 4

1lb (½ kilo) pork sausagemeat
3 cooking apples
1 large onion, chopped
3oz (75gm) white breadcrumbs
1 egg
salt and pepper
2 eating apples
2oz (50gm) butter

1. Preheat oven to moderate to moderately hot, 375 deg F or gas 5 (190 deg C).
2. Roll out sausagemeat on a floured board to about ½ inch thick.
3. Peel, core and dice the apples and mix with onion, breadcrumbs and egg.
4. Season well and spread over the sausagemeat.
5. Roll up like a Swiss roll, put into a buttered casserole and bake in centre of oven for 45 minutes.
6. Peel, core and slice the eating apples into rings. Fry gently in butter and arrange on cooked sausage roll. Serve hot.

HOT HAM
Serves 4

1½oz (37gm) butter
½ teaspoon cayenne pepper
good shake of black pepper
½ teaspoon curry powder
1 teaspoon Worcestershire sauce
1 tomato, skinned and sieved
4 thick slices gammon
2 apples
½ pint (250ml) stock

1. Preheat oven to moderate, 350 deg F or gas 4 (180 deg C).
2. Blend butter, pepper, curry powder, sauce and tomato together.
3. Spread over the gammon.
4. Set gammon on a baking dish and slice the apples over.
5. Add stock, cover and bake in centre of oven for 30 minutes.

EGG AND BACON BAKE
Serves 4

2oz (50gm) boiled bacon
3 hard-boiled eggs
2oz (50gm) mushrooms
2 sticks celery
1½oz (37gm) butter
1½oz (37gm) flour
¾ pint (375ml) milk
salt and pepper
4 tablespoons breadcrumbs

1. Preheat oven to moderate, 350 deg F or gas 4 (180 deg C).
2. Chop bacon and turn into a casserole with the sliced eggs.
3. Chop mushrooms and celery very finely.
4. Cook in butter until tender but not browned.
5. Stir in the flour and then gradually beat in the milk.
6. Season and cook over a medium heat until thickened.
7. Pour over bacon and eggs in the casserole and sprinkle with breadcrumbs.
8. Bake in centre of oven for 15 minutes.

BACON ROLL
Serves 4

1lb (½ kilo) plain flour
½ teaspoon salt
6oz (50gm) shredded suet
8oz (200gm) tomatoes
8oz (200gm) streaky bacon
2 small onions
1 teaspoon dried sage
salt and pepper

1. Sift flour and salt in a bowl.
2. Add suet and mix to a soft pastry dough with water.
3. Turn on to a floured board and roll out to ½ inch thickness.
4. Skin tomatoes and chop roughly.
5. Chop and add bacon and onion. Spread over the suet pastry and sprinkle with sage, salt and pepper.
6. Roll up pastry with the filling inside. Damp and seal the ends.
7. Tie in a floured cloth and boil in a saucepan of water for 2 hours.

LITTLE BACON FLANS
Serves 4

shortcrust pastry made with 8oz (200gm) flour (see Basic recipes, page 100)
4oz (100gm) middle cut bacon rashers
1 medium onion
½oz (12gm) butter
3oz (75gm) cheese, grated
2 eggs
½ pint (250ml) rich milk, or cream and milk together
pepper

1. Preheat oven to moderately hot, 400 deg F or gas 6 (200 deg C).
2. Line four individual patty tins or flan rings, each approximately 4 inches (10cm) in diameter, with the pastry.
3. De-rind the bacon and cut it into small pieces.
4. Fry bacon pieces with finely chopped onion in melted butter.
5. Remove from pan and mix with grated cheese.
6. Divide the mixture between the four prepared pastry cases.
7. Lightly whisk the eggs, milk or milk and cream mixture and pepper.
8. Put the pastry cases on to a baking sheet and carefully spoon the mixture into each case.
9. Bake in the preheated oven for 10 minutes. Reduce heat to moderate, 350 deg F or gas 4 (180 deg C) and cook for a further 25–30 minutes, until pastry is brown and filling set.
10. Serve hot or cold.

CHICKEN CASSEROLE
(Illustrated on page 36)
Serves 4

4 chicken joints
2oz (50gm) plain flour, seasoned
with salt and pepper
2oz (50gm) butter
1 onion, chopped
4 tomatoes, skinned
¾ pint (375ml) chicken stock
2 red peppers, sliced

1. Preheat oven to moderate, 350
deg F or gas 4 (180 deg C).
2. Coat chicken joints in seasoned
flour.
3. Fry on all sides in hot butter
until golden brown. Place in a
casserole.
4. Fry onion in remaining fat.
5. Add with the tomatoes cut into
quarters and chicken stock to the
casserole.
6. Cover and cook in centre of
oven for 1 hour.
7. Add sliced red peppers and
cook for a further 15 minutes.
Serve at once.

MINCED CHICKEN BAKE
Serves 4

6oz (150gm) cooked chicken
2 eggs, separated
salt and pepper
3 mushrooms
2 tablespoons cream
1 tablespoon milk

1. Preheat oven to moderate to
moderately hot, 375 deg F or gas 5
(190 deg C).
2. Chop or very finely mince the
chicken.
3. Mix in egg yolks and season
very well.
4. Chop and add mushrooms.
5. Whip the cream until just
lightly thickened and add, with
whisked egg whites, to the
chicken mixture.
6. Add milk, spoon into a
buttered pie dish and bake in
centre of oven for 20 minutes, or
until well browned and risen.
Serve at once.

PIQUANT CHICKEN IN
TOMATO
Serves 4

2 tablespoons olive oil
4 chicken joints
1 head of celery
8oz (200gm) bacon, cut into
2-inch slices
1 dozen bottled silverskin
onions
1 large can cream of tomato
soup
salt and pepper

1. Preheat oven to very moderate,
325 deg F or gas 3 (170 deg C).
2. Heat oil and fry chicken until
golden brown. Drain.
3. Chop celery and blanch it.
4. Fry bacon until brown.
5. Place chicken, celery, bacon
and onions in a casserole and
cover with tomato soup.
6. Season to taste and bake in
centre of oven for about 1 hour.

CHICKEN CREOLE
Serves 4

4 cooked chicken joints
1 onion
1 green pepper
oil for frying
8oz (200gm) mushrooms
1 can (8oz or 200gm) tomatoes
1 can (7oz or 175gm) pineapple
tidbits
2 tablespoons vinegar
1 dessertspoon brown sugar
2 tablespoons soy sauce
1 tablespoon cornflour

1. Preheat oven to moderate to
moderately hot, 375 deg F or gas 5
(190 deg C).
2. Place chicken joints in a
fireproof casserole.
3. Fry onion and pepper in oil.
Add remaining ingredients and
thicken with cornflour.
4. Pour over chicken and cook in
centre of oven for 30 minutes.
5. Serve on a bed of rice or
noodles.

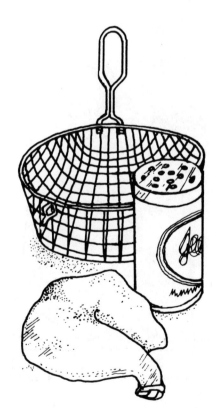

CHICKEN PIE SUPREME
Serves 4

2 cooked chicken joints
8oz (200gm) cooked pork
sausages
2 tomatoes
1 can (10½oz or 262gm)
condensed cream of celery
soup
1 tablespoon milk
1 packet (7½oz or 187gm) frozen
shortcrust pastry (or see Basic
recipes, page 100)

1. Preheat oven to moderately
hot, 400 deg F or gas 6 (200 deg C).
2. Remove meat from chicken
joints and slice sausages at an
angle.
3. Roughly chop tomatoes.
4. Place soup in a bowl with milk
and add chicken, sausages and
tomatoes. Stir thoroughly until
well mixed.
4. Turn into a 9-inch (23cm)
ovenproof pie plate. Roll out
pastry and cover pie.
5. Brush with milk and bake in
centre of oven for 40 minutes.

COD WITH MUSTARD SAUCE
Serves 4

4 small cod fillets
½oz (12gm) cornflour, seasoned
with salt and pepper
3 tablespoons corn oil
1 large packet frozen
vegetables
½ pint (250ml) white sauce (see
Basic recipes, page 100)
3 tablespoons cream
2 level tablespoons mustard,
mixed with a little vinegar

1. Skin the cod fillets and coat
well with seasoned cornflour.
2. Heat corn oil and fry the fish
on both sides until cooked.
3. Cook the frozen vegetables in
boiling, salted water. Drain, and
place in a serving dish. Place fish
on top.
4. Make up white sauce, remove
from heat and stir in cream and
mustard.
5. Pour the sauce over the fish
and serve at once.

COD BAKE
Serves 4–6

1½lb (¾ kilo) cod fillet, cut into
pieces
salt and pepper
1oz (25gm) flour
2oz (50gm) butter
1 large onion, peeled and sliced
1 large can mushroom soup
1 tablespoon white
breadcrumbs
2oz (50gm) Cheddar cheese,
grated

1. Preheat oven to moderate to
moderately hot, 375 deg F or gas 5
(190 deg C).
2. Sprinkle fish with salt and
pepper, dip in flour and fry gently
in butter to brown slightly.
Transfer to a shallow dish.
3. Fry onion in same pan for 5
minutes. Add to fish.
4. Pour soup over fish and
onions, sprinkle with
breadcrumbs and cheese and bake
in centre of oven for 30 minutes.
Serve hot.

MERMAID'S SUPPER
Serves 4

1½lb (¾ kilo) white fish
salt and pepper
5oz (125gm) butter
1½oz (37gm) flour
½ pint (250ml) milk
6oz (150gm) Gruyère cheese,
grated
12oz (300gm) mushrooms

1. Preheat oven to moderate to
moderately hot, 375 deg F or gas 5
(190 deg C).
2. Put the cleaned, skinned and
boned fish into a pan with just
enough water or fish stock to
cover.
3. Season, cover with a lid and
cook until fish is cooked and
flakes easily.
4. Melt 1½oz (37gm) butter in a
pan and stir in flour, add milk,
season and bring to the boil.
5. Stir in cheese and flaked fish.
6. Put this mixture into individual
ovenware dishes.
7. Slice and fry mushrooms in
remaining butter and heap these
on top of each dish.
8. Cover and bake in centre of
oven for 10 minutes.

PLAICE WITH SWEETCORN
Serves 4

8 plaice fillets
1 egg, beaten
6oz (150gm) quick-cooking oats
4oz (100gm) butter
1 onion, chopped
4oz (100gm) mushrooms, sliced
1 medium can sweetcorn

1. Dip the fillets in egg and coat with oats.
2. Melt butter in a large pan and fry onion and mushrooms.
3. Grill the fish on each side.
4. Add drained sweetcorn to the onion and mushroom and heat through.
5. Put vegetables on a large dish, pour remaining butter over and serve the grilled fish on top.

SEA TREAT
Serves 4

salt and pepper
4 plaice fillets
4 streaky bacon rashers
¼ pint (125ml) milk
¼ pint (125ml) fish stock
1oz (25gm) butter
1oz (25gm) flour
2oz (50gm) cheese, grated
parsley to garnish

1. Preheat oven to moderate, 350 deg F or gas 4 (180 deg C).
2. Season the fillets.
3. Remove bacon rinds and put 1 rasher on each fillet.
4. Roll up carefully and put in a buttered pie dish.
5. Pour over milk and stock and bake in centre of oven for 15–20 minutes.
6. Heat butter in a pan and mix in flour.
7. Remove from heat and beat in the milk and stock drained from the fish.
8. Season, add cheese and cook, stirring until thick.
9. Pour over fish and serve garnished with parsley.

MUSTARD FISH
Serves 4

1½lb (¾ kilo) hake, skinned
1 tablespoon made mustard
pinch of grated nutmeg
pinch of marjoram
salt and pepper
2oz (50gm) butter

1. Preheat oven to moderate, 350 deg F or gas 4 (180 deg C).
2. Spread fish on all sides with mustard, then place it in a greased dish.
3. Sprinkle with herbs and seasoning and dot with butter.
4. Cover closely and bake in centre of oven for 40 minutes, basting occasionally during cooking.
5. Serve with creamed potatoes and a green vegetable.

POACHED HERRINGS WITH MUSHROOMS
Serves 4

4 herrings
12oz (300gm) mushrooms
salt and pepper
6 peppercorns
1 bayleaf
½ pint (250ml) cider or fish stock
½oz (12gm) butter
sprigs of parsley

1. Preheat oven to moderate to moderately hot, 375 deg F or gas 5 (190 deg C).
2. Put the cleaned herrings into a large casserole and arrange mushrooms round the edge.
3. Season with salt and pepper and add peppercorns and bayleaf to casserole.
4. Pour cider or stock over.
5. Cover with a lid or kitchen foil and bake in centre of oven for about 20 minutes or until ingredients are tender and evenly cooked.
6. Arrange fish on a hot serving dish, dot with butter and edge with the mushrooms. Garnish with parsley.
7. Serve fish hot with potatoes or cold with a green salad.

INSTANT PILCHARD SUPPER
Serves 4

1lb (½ kilo) long-grain rice
2 pints (approximately 1 litre) water
2 teaspoons salt
1 oz (50gm) butter
1 onion, chopped
salt and pepper
1 tomato, chopped
1 can pilchards in tomato sauce
parsley

1. Put rice, water and salt into a saucepan, bring to the boil and stir once.
2. Lower heat to simmer. Cover tightly and cook for 15 minutes or until rice is tender and liquid absorbed.
3. Melt butter in a deep pan. Stir in onion, salt and pepper.
4. When onion is soft, stir in chopped tomato.
5. Split pilchards in half and break them into bite-sized pieces. Add to onion and tomato.
6. Stir cooked rice into fried onion mixture and keep stirring gently until it is thoroughly warm.
7. Garnish with parsley and serve with hot rolls or toast.

CRISPY KIPPER ROLL
Serves 4

1 packet frozen kipper fillets
2oz (50gm) butter, softened
2 teaspoons lemon juice
salt and pepper
1 French loaf
lemon wedges to garnish

1. Preheat oven to moderately hot, 400 deg F or gas 6 (200 deg C).
2. Cook kipper fillets according to instructions on packet.
3. Drain, remove skin and flake fish.
4. Pound together fish, butter and lemon juice until smooth and season well.
5. Cut French loaf into 1-inch thick slices, to within $\frac{1}{2}$ inch of the bottom.
6. Press a little kipper mixture between each slice, re-form the loaf and wrap in foil.
7. Bake in oven for 15 minutes.
8. Serve hot, garnished with lemon wedges.

PRAWN AND EGG FLAN
Serves 4

shortcrust pastry made with 4oz (100gm) flour (see Basic recipes, page 100)
2$\frac{1}{2}$oz (62gm) butter or margarine
1$\frac{1}{2}$oz (37gm) flour
$\frac{1}{2}$ pint (250ml) milk
salt and pepper
4oz (100gm) frozen prawns, thawed
4 eggs

1. Preheat oven to moderately hot, 400 deg F or gas 6 (200 deg C).
2. Roll out pastry to line a 7-inch (20cm) flan case.
3. Prick and line with greaseproof paper and fill with baking beans.
4. Bake in centre of oven for 10 minutes, then remove baking beans and paper and cook for a further 10 minutes.
5. Melt 1$\frac{1}{2}$oz (37gm) butter in a pan, stir in the flour and cook for a moment. Beat in the milk and seasoning. Stirring, bring to the boil.
6. Stir in the prawns and spoon into the flan case.
7. Break eggs on top of the flan and dot yolks with remaining butter or margarine.
8. Bake in centre of oven for 20 minutes until the eggs are set. Serve hot.

TUNA SUPPER DISH
Serves 4

2 cans tuna steak
2 tablespoons olive oil
1 large or 2 small aubergines, cut into $\frac{1}{4}$-inch slices, sprinkled with salt and left for 30 minutes
1 large onion, skinned and sliced
1 medium can tomatoes
1 garlic clove, crushed with a little salt
pinch each of basil, thyme and marjoram
salt and pepper
2 egg yolks
$\frac{1}{2}$ pint (250ml) milk

1. Preheat oven to moderate to moderately hot, 375 deg F or gas 5 (190 deg C).
2. Put the oil from the tuna and the olive oil into a frying pan and fry drained aubergine slices quickly.
3. Put them on one side and fry the onion until transparent.
4. Add tomatoes, garlic, herbs and seasoning.
5. Fill a deep casserole dish with alternate layers of aubergines, tomato mixture and pieces of tuna.
6. Finish with a layer of aubergines.
7. Beat the egg yolks and milk together with a fork, season and pour into dish.
8. Bake in centre of oven for 45 minutes.

TUNA FISH PILAF
Serves 4

2 tablespoons oil
1 large onion, finely sliced
8oz (200gm) long-grain rice
salt and pepper
1$\frac{1}{2}$ pints ($\frac{3}{4}$ litre) chicken stock
$\frac{1}{2}$oz (12gm) butter
8oz (200gm) mushrooms
squeeze of lemon juice
1 can tuna fish, flaked

1. Heat oil in a pan, add onion and cook until it is soft.
2. Add rice and fry for a few minutes until rice is transparent.
3. Season and add stock. Bring to the boil, cover tightly and simmer for 20 minutes.
4. Melt butter in a pan and add mushrooms and lemon juice. Toss over a brisk heat for 2 minutes, then fork in tuna fish. Season and cook for a further 2 minutes.
5. Put rice mixture into a ring mould and press lightly with a plate to make rice hold together.
6. Turn out on to a serving dish and fill centre with tuna fish and mushrooms.

TUNA AND EGG PLAIT
Serves 4

1 packet (13oz or 325gm) frozen puff pastry (or see Basic recipes, page 100)
1 packet white sauce mix
$\frac{1}{2}$ pint (250ml) milk
1 can (7oz or 175gm) tuna, drained
2 hard-boiled eggs
salt and pepper
2 tomatoes
1 egg, beaten

1. Preheat oven to hot, 425 deg F or gas 7 (220 deg C).
2. Roll out pastry to an oblong, about 12 inches by 10 inches.
3. Make up white sauce with milk, following directions on the packet, and add to it the tuna, flaked with a fork.
4. Add chopped eggs and season to taste.
5. Arrange this filling down centre of pastry and top with tomato slices. Moisten pastry sides.
6. Cut pastry sides into $\frac{1}{2}$-inch strips, slantways, and plait these alternately over the top of the filling.
7. Brush with egg and bake in centre of oven for 25 minutes.

FRICASSEE OF SALMON
Serves 2–4

½ pint (250ml) stock or water
½ pint (250ml) milk
2 cloves
1 small onion, quartered
1 small bayleaf
1 blade of mace
1 sprig of parsley
1 level teaspoon salt
1oz (25gm) butter
1oz (25gm) flour
8oz (200gm) button mushrooms
2 cans (7½oz or 187gm each)
salmon, flaked in large pieces
salt and pepper
lemon wedges and chopped
parsley to garnish

1. Pour stock or water and milk
into a saucepan
2. Add cloves, onion, bayleaf,
mace, parsley and salt and bring
to the boil.
3. Lower heat, cover and simmer
for 20 minutes. Strain liquor and
reserve.
4. Melt butter in a clean saucepan
and stir in flour. Cook gently for
2 minutes, stirring continuously.
5. Remove pan from heat and
gradually blend in liquor. Cook,
stirring, until sauce boils and
thickens.
6. Add mushrooms and simmer
for 5 minutes.
7. Add salmon and simmer for a
further 3 minutes.
8. Season to taste and serve
immediately, garnished with
lemon wedges and parsley.

LENTIL CAKES
Serves 4

8oz (200gm) lentils
1oz (25gm) butter
1 onion, chopped
1½ pints (approximately ¾ litre)
water
salt and pepper
4 tablespoons ground rice
2 tablespoons chopped parsley
1 egg, beaten
breadcrumbs
fat for deep frying

1. Wash lentils.
2. Melt butter in a saucepan and
toss lentils and onion in it until
fat is absorbed.
3. Add water and seasoning and
simmer for about 1 hour, until
lentils are soft.
4. Add ground rice and cook for
10 minutes. Add parsley and turn
out on to a plate. Leave to cool.
5. Shape into 8 round cakes, coat
in egg and crumbs.
6. Fry, drain and serve hot with
baked tomatoes.

SCALLOPED ONIONS
Serves 4

4 onions
½oz (12gm) butter
½oz (12gm) cornflour
½ pint (250ml) milk
salt and pepper
½oz (12gm) breadcrumbs
2oz (50gm) cheese, grated
4 back bacon rashers

1. Skin the onions and boil in a
pan of water until tender.
2. Drain them and keep hot in a
fireproof dish.
3. Melt butter in a pan and add
cornflour.
4. Blend in the milk, season and
cook for a few minutes until
thickened.
5. Pour over the onions and
sprinkle with breadcrumbs and
cheese.
6. Brown under the grill.
7. Grill bacon separately and
arrange on top of the dish.

ITALIAN RISOTTO
Serves 4

2oz (50gm) butter
1 small onion, finely chopped
8oz (200gm) long-grain rice
½ teaspoon saffron
ground nutmeg
1 teaspoon salt
¼ teaspoon pepper
1 pint (approximately ½ litre)
boiling stock
1 tablespoon tomato purée
2oz (50gm) grated Parmesan
cheese

1. Heat butter in a saucepan, add
onion and cook until lightly
browned.
2. Add rice and shake pan over
heat for about 10 minutes.
3. Sprinkle in saffron, a good
pinch of nutmeg, salt and pepper.
4. Add stock and bring to the
boil. Stir once.
5. Lower heat and simmer,
covered, for about 15 minutes,
until rice is tender and liquid
absorbed.
6. Add tomato purée and blend
thoroughly.
7. Just before serving, stir in the
cheese.

CELERY AU GRATIN
Serves 4

2oz (50gm) butter or margarine
1 can celery hearts
1oz (25gm) flour
a little milk
salt and pepper
4oz (100gm) cheese, grated
few breadcrumbs

1. Melt the butter or margarine gently and heat the drained celery in it. Reserve liquid. Remove celery and arrange in a heatproof dish.
2. Add flour to the butter and gradually stir in the celery liquid, made up to ½ pint (250ml) with milk. Stirring, bring to the boil.
3. Season well and add 2½oz (62gm) cheese.
4. Coat celery with this sauce and sprinkle with cheese and breadcrumbs.
5. Brown under a very hot grill and serve with fried sausages or fried slices of luncheon meat.

BEAN AND POTATO PIE
Serves 4

4oz (100gm) cheese, grated
1 teaspoon made mustard
1lb (½ kilo) mashed potatoes
1 large onion, peeled and chopped
4oz (100gm) streaky bacon, de-rinded and cut into pieces
4 tomatoes, skinned and sliced
1 large can baked beans

1. Preheat oven to hot, 425 deg F or gas 7 (220 deg C).
2. Mix cheese and mustard into the mashed potatoes.
3. Fry onion, bacon and tomatoes, reserving a few slices of tomato for garnish.
4. Add baked beans and heat through.
5. Place mixture in an ovenware casserole dish.
6. Pipe the potato mixture in lattice decoration or pile on and mark with a fork.
7. Bake for 15 minutes on centre shelf.

SPANISH BAKED BEANS
Serves 4

2 streaky bacon rashers
1 garlic clove, crushed
1 tablespoon tomato ketchup
1 level tablespoon paprika
pinch of marjoram
2 medium cans baked beans
2 pork sausages, cooked and chopped
4 eggs

1. Preheat oven to moderate to moderately hot, 375 deg F or gas 5 (190 deg C).
2. Rind and cut the bacon into strips. Cook lightly with the garlic.
3. Add tomato ketchup, paprika and marjoram.
4. Put baked beans and sausages in an ovenware dish. Place bacon mixture on top.
5. Spoon four hollows in the beans and break an egg into each.
6. Cover and bake in centre of oven for about 20 minutes, or until the eggs are set.

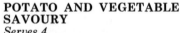

POTATOES DE LUXE
Serves 4–6

1½lb (¾ kilo) potatoes
4 tablespoons dry white wine
4oz (100gm) streaky bacon
2 onions, sliced
½ green pepper, chopped
4oz (100gm) mushrooms, sliced
1oz (25gm) butter
salt and pepper
4oz (100gm) Cheddar cheese, grated
chopped parsley to garnish

1. Preheat oven to hot, 425 deg F or gas 7 (220 deg C).
2. Peel the potatoes and cook in boiling, salted water for 10–15 minutes.
3. Drain, cut into slices and lay in the bottom of a pie dish.
4. Pour the wine over.
5. Rind and cut the bacon into small pieces.
6. Cook with onions, green pepper and mushrooms in melted butter until tender.
7. Season to taste and spoon mixture over the potatoes.
8. Sprinkle with grated cheese and cook on centre shelf of oven for 15 minutes.
9. Serve sprinkled with parsley.

POTATO AND VEGETABLE SAVOURY
Serves 4

1½lb (¾ kilo) potatoes
1 onion
1 large carrot
2 level tablespoons chopped parsley
1 large can condensed vegetable or celery soup
4oz (100gm) cheese, grated
salt and pepper
½oz (12gm) butter

1. Peel the potatoes, onion and carrot, then slice and cook.
2. Mash them together and add parsley, soup and 3oz (75gm) cheese. Season to taste.
3. Butter an ovenware dish and put the potato mixture in it.
4. Sprinkle with remaining cheese and brown under a hot grill, or in a hot oven.

MUSHROOM SOUFFLE
Serves 4

3oz (75gm) butter
2oz (50gm) flour
½ pint (250ml) hot milk
2 tablespoons grated Parmesan
cheese
salt and cayenne pepper
pinch of grated nutmeg
1 onion, finely chopped
8oz (200gm) mushrooms, thinly
sliced
4 egg yolks
5 egg whites

1. Preheat oven to moderate, 350 deg F or gas 4 (180 deg C).
2. Melt 2oz (50gm) butter in a pan. Add flour and cook until flour just starts to turn brown.
3. Mix in milk and cook, stirring constantly with a whisk, until sauce is thick and smooth.
4. Add Parmesan, salt, cayenne pepper and grated nutmeg to taste.
5. Fry onion in remaining butter until it is transparent. Add mushrooms and cook until all the moisture has evaporated.
6. Add onions and mushrooms to hot sauce.
7. Beat egg yolks and fold into sauce mixture.
8. Beat egg whites until they are just stiff and fold into mixture.
9. Fill a buttered dish about three-quarters full and bake in centre of oven for about 40 minutes. Serve at once.

MUSHROOM PUFF
Serves 4

1 can (15½oz or 387gm)
mushroom soup
1 rounded tablespoon cornflour
3 eggs, separated

1. Preheat oven to moderate, 350 deg or gas 4 (180 deg C).
2. Blend soup with cornflour.
3. Mix in 3 egg yolks, stirring well.
4. Whisk egg whites until stiff and fold into mushroom soup mixture with a metal spoon.
5. Pour into a deep, ovenware bowl and bake in centre of oven for 30 minutes until risen and golden.

TOMATO SUPPER DISH
Serves 4

salt and pepper
1½lb (¾ kilo) mashed potato
6 eggs
4 tablespoons milk
1–2 level tablespoons sage and
onion stuffing mixture
1 medium can tomatoes
3oz (75gm) cheese, grated

1. Preheat oven to moderate to moderately hot, 375 deg F or gas 5 (190 deg C).
2. Beat seasoning into mashed potato and add 1 egg.
3. Beat in the milk to make a creamy mixture. Pile around a buttered, fireproof dish.
4. Sprinkle with seasoning and stuffing mixture.
5. Tip tomatoes into centre of fireproof dish and break remaining eggs over the top.
6. Cover with cheese and bake in centre of oven for 20 minutes until eggs are just set.
7. Serve hot with a green vegetable.

TOMATO RISOTTO
Serves 4

1oz (25gm) butter
2oz (50gm) rice
4oz (100gm) tomato pulp or
cooking tomatoes
2 tablespoons chopped onion
8oz (200gm) cold meat, diced
1 packet tomato soup, made
with 1 pint (approximately ½
litre) water
salt and pepper
2oz (50gm) cheese, grated

1. Melt butter, add rice and fry for 2 minutes.
2. Add tomato pulp or cooking tomatoes and onion. Cook for a further 2 minutes.
3. Mix in the meat, tomato soup and salt and pepper to taste.
4. Cover with a lid and simmer gently for about 15 minutes until rice is tender and liquid all absorbed.
5. Serve hot with cheese sprinkled on top.

TOMATO CRISP
Serves 4

1oz (25gm) butter
6 medium tomatoes
2oz (50gm) cheese, grated
1½oz (37gm) breadcrumbs
salt and pepper

1. Preheat oven to moderate, 350 deg F or gas 4 (180 deg C).
2. Butter a pie dish with 1½oz (12gm) butter.
3. Slice the tomatoes.
4. Mix cheese with breadcrumbs and put in the pie dish.
5. Cover with a layer of tomatoes. Fill up the dish in this way, seasoning well and finishing with a layer of breadcrumbs.
6. Top with dabs of remaining butter and bake in centre of oven for 30 minutes.

SUPPER A LA ROMA
Serves 4

**2 medium cans spaghetti in
tomato sauce
1 onion, skinned and sliced
4oz (100gm) ham, cut into strips
1 aubergine, sliced into rings
2oz (50gm) cheese, grated
4oz (100gm) mushrooms**

1. Preheat oven to very moderate,
325 deg F or gas 3 (170 deg C).
2. Mix spaghetti, onion rings,
ham strips and aubergine rings
carefully together.
3. Place half the spaghetti mix on
the base of a 10-inch (25cm)
ovenware dish and cover with
grated cheese.
4. Top with rest of spaghetti mix,
cover with foil and place in centre
of oven for 35 minutes.
5. Meanwhile, lightly grill the
mushrooms and arrange round the
edge of dish.
6. Serve with a tossed green
salad.

CHEESE PUDDING
Serves 4

**2 small eggs, separated
½ pint (250ml) warm milk
2½oz (62gm) Cheddar cheese,
grated
2 teaspoons chopped parsley
¼ teaspoon mustard
1 teaspoon salt
2oz (50gm) white breadcrumbs
pinch of salt**

1. Preheat oven to moderately
hot, 400 deg F or gas 6 (200 deg C).
2. Butter a 2-pint (approximately
1 litre) dish.
3. Blend egg yolks with warm
milk, cheese and parsley.
4. Season well with mustard and
salt.
5. Pour over the breadcrumbs
and leave until cold.
6. Whisk egg whites with a pinch
of salt until they stand stiffly in
peaks. Fold gently into
breadcrumb mixture.
7. Pour into prepared dish and
bake on second shelf from top of
oven for 30 minutes. Serve at
once.

CHEESE SQUARES
(Illustrated on page 36)
Serves 4

Cheese and semolina mixture cut
into squares and baked until
crisp.

**2 pints (approximately 1 litre)
milk
8oz (200gm) semolina
4oz (100gm) cheese, grated
3oz (75gm) butter
2 egg yolks
salt and pepper
4 tomatoes
sprigs of watercress**

1. Preheat oven to moderately
hot, 400 deg F or gas 6 (200 deg C).
2. Bring milk to the boil and
sprinkle in the semolina.
3. Stir over a gentle heat for 10
minutes until thickened.
4. Remove from heat and stir in
3oz (75gm) grated cheese.
5. Add ½oz (12gm) butter and egg
yolks. Season well.
6. Spread out on a plate and
leave to get cold. Cut into 1-inch
squares.
7. Fill a pie dish with the squares
and tomato slices and top with
rest of cheese.
8. Bake in centre of oven dotted
with remaining butter for 15
minutes.
9. Garnish with watercress and
serve at once.

CHEESE PASTRY SLICE
Serves 4

A pastry turnover with a cheese
and oat filling.

**shortcrust pastry made with
12oz (300gm) flour (see Basic
recipes, page 100)
8oz (100gm) rolled oats
4oz (100gm) cheese, grated
1 dessertspoon made mustard
1 tablespoon water
salt and pepper
1oz (25gm) butter**

1. Preheat oven to moderately
hot, 400 deg F or gas 6 (200 deg C).
2. Roll out pastry on a floured
board and use half of it to line a
baking tin.
3. Mix oats with cheese, mustard
water, salt and pepper.
4. Melt the butter and spread over
the pastry lining the tin. Add oats
and cheese filling.
5. Damp the edges of pastry and
cover with remaining piece of
pastry.
6. Seal edges well and bake in
centre of oven for 30 minutes.
Cut into slices to serve.

FARMHOUSE PIE
Serves 4

**shortcrust pastry made with
8oz (200gm) flour (see Basic
recipes, page 100)
4oz (100gm) streaky bacon
3 eggs
½ pint (250ml) milk
salt and pepper**

1. Preheat oven to moderately
hot, 400 deg F or gas 6 (200 deg C).
2. Roll out two thirds of the
pastry to line a 7-inch (18cm) pie
plate.
3. Remove rinds, chop the bacon
and spread over pastry case.
4. Whisk eggs and milk and pour
on to the bacon. Sprinkle with
salt and pepper.
5. Damp pastry edge. Roll out
rest of pastry to make a lid and
place carefully on top of pie.
6. Seal edges well together, make
a slit in the top and brush with
milk.
7. Bake in centre of oven for
30–35 minutes. Serve hot with
vegetables or cold with salad.

Speedy goulash (see page 57) Piquant turkey legs (see page 60)

Egg scramble (see page 63) Farmhouse supper dish (see page 64)

Apple salads topped with a walnut (see page 73)   Liver pâté (see page 67)

Salami and cheese cornets on a bed of lettuce (see page 66)   Jellied tomatoes (see page 73)

CHEESE AND CHICKEN FLAN
Serves 4

shortcrust pastry made with
4oz (100gm) flour (see Basic
recipes, page 100)
1 onion
2oz (50gm) butter
1 can celery
1oz (25gm) flour
½ pint (250ml) milk or celery
stock
salt and pepper
4oz (100gm) cooked chicken,
chopped
1½oz (37gm) cheese, grated

1. Preheat oven to moderately
hot, 400 deg F or gas 6 (200 deg C).
2. Roll out pastry and use to line
a 7-inch (18cm) flan ring.
3. Line with greaseproof paper
and fill with dry haricot beans.
Bake in centre of oven for 15
minutes. Remove beans and cook
for a further 15 minutes.
4. Peel and slice onion and fry in
half the butter until golden brown.
5. Chop celery and add to onion.
6. Make a white sauce with
remaining butter, the flour and
liquid. Bring to the boil and pour
over the vegetables.
7. Season and add chopped
chicken and half the cheese. Fill
flan case with this mixture.
8. Cover with remaining cheese
and brown under a hot grill.
Serve hot or cold.

EGGS CREOLE
Serves 4

1 large onion
4 tablespoons chopped green
pepper
2oz (50gm) lard
1 pint (approximately ½ litre)
water
1lb (½ kilo) tomatoes, skinned
6oz (150gm) rice
salt and pepper
4 eggs

1. Cook onion and green pepper
in lard in a large frying pan until
onion is slightly browned.
2. Add water and tomatoes and
heat until boiling.
3. Add rice and seasoning and
cook over a low heat for about 20
minutes, until rice is tender.
4. Stir occasionally with a fork to
prevent sticking and add a little
more water if it becomes too dry.
5. Put into a hot pie dish, poach
the eggs and put on top.

STUFFED SUPPER EGGS
Serves 4

Hard-boiled eggs with a cheese
and onion stuffing and served on a
cabbage base.

1 small cabbage
3oz (75gm) butter
¼ pint (125ml) stock
salt and pepper
¾oz (18gm) flour
½ pint (250ml) milk
1oz (25gm) cheese, grated
½ teaspoon English mustard
1 small onion, chopped
4 hard-boiled eggs

1. Cut cabbage into four and
discard the thick stalk.
2. Wash well and plunge the
cabbage pieces into a pan of
boiling water for 1 minute, then
drain it.
3. Turn into a pan with 1oz
(25gm) butter and the stock.
4. Season, put a lid on the pan
and cook over a very low heat for
about 15 minutes until cabbage is
tender.
5. Melt 1oz (25gm) butter, stir in
the flour and cook for a moment.
6. Beat in ¼ pint (125ml) milk,
bring to the boil and stir in cheese
and mustard.
7. Cook onion in rest of the
butter.
8. Split eggs, scoop out yolks and
sieve. Mix with onion and 2
tablespoons of the sauce.
9. Spoon filling into the egg
whites.
10. Add rest of milk to cheese
sauce and reheat.
11. Set eggs on the cabbage on a
hot plate and coat with sauce.
Sprinkle with a little extra cheese
and grill until golden.

COUNTRY EGGS
Serves 4

2 medium potatoes,
2 carrots
2 tomatoes, skinned
3 pork sausages, cooked
4oz (100gm) runner beans
salt and pepper
¼ pint (125ml) meat stock
4 eggs
1oz (25gm) Cheddar cheese,
grated

1. Preheat oven to moderately
hot, 400 deg F or gas 6 (200 deg C).
2. Peel the potatoes and dice.
3. Scrape and grate the carrots.
Cook both in a pan of boiling,
salted water for 5 minutes.
4. Drain and turn into a casserole.
Add sliced tomatoes and sausages.
5. String and slice the beans and
add to the casserole. Season well
and pour in the stock.
6. Break the eggs into hollows in
the vegetables. Sprinkle with
cheese.
7. Bake in centre of oven for 20
minutes or until the eggs have
just set. Serve at once.

EGGS BOMBAY
Serves 4

8 eggs
1 large onion, chopped
2 tablespoons cooking oil
1oz (25gm) flour
1 level tablespoon curry powder
1 medium can pineapple cubes
1 tablespoon chutney
salt
6oz (150gm) long-grain rice

1. Hard-boil eggs and shell them.
2. Peel and chop onion.
3. Fry in oil until tender and just
beginning to brown.
4. Mix in flour and curry and
cook gently for 2–3 minutes.
5. Strain the pineapple, make up
juice with water to 1 pint
(approximately ½ litre) and stir
into the pan.
6. Add most of the pineapple
cubes, chutney and salt. Simmer
for about 20 minutes, stirring
occasionally.
7. Cook rice in boiling, salted
water for 12 minutes, then strain.
8. Cut eggs in half lengthways,
add them to curry sauce and heat
through.
9. Serve curried eggs bordered
with rice. Garnish with remaining
pineapple cubes.

Suppers in a hurry

If you have had a busy day or you are going out for the evening you don't want to spend ages on preparing a meal. These recipes should just fit the bill.

QUICK ONION SOUP
Serves 4

1 packet onion soup mix
1½ pints (approximately ¾ litre) water
1 French loaf
2oz (50gm) cheese, grated

1. Make up onion soup as directed on the packet with water.
2. While the soup is cooking, cut bread in slices, sprinkle with cheese and toast lightly under the grill.
3. Pour soup into serving plates and float two or three slices of toast in each. Serve at once.

FRANKFURTERS WITH SOUP
Serves 4

1 packet green pea soup
1½ pints (approximately ¾ litre) water
4–6 frankfurter sausages, sliced

1. Make up the soup as directed on the packet with water and simmer for 10 minutes.
2. Stir in the frankfurters and heat through. Serve with crusty French bread.

CHEESE EGGBURGERS
Serves 4

4 frozen beefburgers
4 bap rolls
4 eggs
1 packet cheese sauce mix
½ pint (250ml) milk

1. Grill beefburgers until cooked through.
2. While they are cooking, split the baps and toast the insides.
3. Poach eggs in boiling, salted water.
4. While they are poaching, make up cheese sauce with milk as directed on the packet.
5. Place one beefburger and one egg in each bap and pour the cheese sauce over the filled baps.

MUSTARD MEAT FRITTERS
Serves 4

6 spring onions, chopped
1oz (25gm) butter
12oz (300gm) cooked beef, minced
1 dessertspoon flour
1 heaped teaspoon dry mustard
salt and pepper
1 egg yolk
¾ pint (375ml) pancake batter (see Basic recipes, page 100)
fat for frying

1. Fry onion in butter.
2. Mix together meat, fried onion, flour, mustard, salt and pepper.
3. Bind with egg yolk, form into eight flat, round cakes and coat with batter.
4. Shallow-fry in fat for about 8 minutes, until golden brown on both sides.
5. Drain on soft kitchen paper and serve with a green vegetable.

SPEEDY GOULASH
(Illustrated on page 53)
Serves 4

1 medium can stewing steak
1 medium can tomatoes
1 small can red peppers,
chopped
1 teaspoon paprika
1 small can mushrooms
5oz (150gm) boiled long-grain
rice (raw weight)
1 carton natural yogurt

1. Heat the stewing steak with
tomatoes and red peppers.
2. Stir in paprika pepper and
bring to the boil.
3. Serve in a hot dish with heated
mushrooms mixed with rice.
4. Accompany with yogurt.

POTATO AND BEEF CAKE
Serves 4

1lb (½ kilo) potatoes, peeled and
grated
1lb (½ kilo) raw minced beef
1 egg
1 teaspoon Worcestershire
sauce
1 medium onion, grated
salt and pepper

1. Mix the potato and meat
together.
2. Add egg, Worcestershire sauce,
onion, salt and pepper.
3. Fry in the shape of a flat scone
until browned underneath.
4. Mark into four sections. Turn
over carefully and cook other
side.
5. Serve piping hot.

CORNED BEEF SPECIAL
Serves 4

1lb (½ kilo) potatoes, parboiled
1 medium can corned beef,
cubed
salt and pepper
1 tablespoon chopped onion
2 eggs
1 tablespoon tomato purée
4 tablespoons very hot water
1 teaspoon chopped parsley

1. Dice and mix potatoes with
corned beef, salt, pepper and
onion, and place in a well-greased
frying pan.
2. Beat eggs until blended.
3. Blend tomato purée with hot
water. Add to eggs, beat well and
pour on to meat mixture.
4. Fry gently for about 15
minutes, stirring occasionally.
5. Sprinkle with parsley and serve
hot.

QUICK BEEF SUPPERS
Serves 4

4 slices bread
1 large onion or 2 tomatoes
salt and pepper
pinch of sugar
1 can corned beef or minced
beef loaf
butter
1 packet cheese sauce mix
½ pint (250ml) milk

1. Toast bread on one side.
2. Slice onions or tomatoes and
sprinkle with a little salt, pepper
and sugar. Fry until tender and
keep hot.
3. Divide corned beef or beef loaf
into 4 thick slices.
4. Lightly butter untoasted side
of the bread and cover with fried
onion or tomato.
5. Place a slice of meat on top of
each and grill until meat sizzles.
6. Meanwhile, make up cheese
sauce as directed on the packet
with milk.
7. Pour cheese sauce over the
meat slices and serve piping hot.

SAVOURY FRIED PORK
Serves 4

1lb (½ kilo) shoulder or leg of
pork, cut into thin slices
salt and pepper
1 egg, beaten
1 packet sage and onion
stuffing
1oz (25gm) lard

1. Flatten the slices of pork with
a rolling pin.
2. Coat each slice with beaten
egg seasoned with salt and pepper
and dry stuffing mixture.
3. Fry in hot lard on both sides
until brown and tender.

QUICKIE HOTPOT
Serves 4

1 packet oxtail soup mix
1 pint (approximately ½ litre)
water
4 chipolata sausages, grilled
and sliced thickly
3oz (75gm) cooked ham
3oz (75gm) cooked turkey or
chicken, diced
2oz (50gm) cooked peas
3 sticks celery, finely chopped
1 dessert apple, chopped

1. Make up oxtail soup with
water as directed on the packet.
2. Add all other ingredients and
cook for a further 5 minutes.
3. Serve with slices of crusty
French bread.

VEAL WITH YOGURT
Serves 4

4 veal fillets
1½oz (37gm) flour
1 egg
4oz (100gm) white breadcrumbs
2oz (50gm) butter
watercress
1 carton natural yogurt

1. Beat the fillets until thin, dust
with flour and coat with beaten
egg and breadcrumbs.
2. Fry on both sides in the hot
butter.
3. Arrange the veal on a hot dish.
Garnish with watercress and
serve the yogurt separately.

FRYING PAN SPECIAL
Serves 4

1lb (½ kilo) potatoes, peeled
and parboiled
1 medium can luncheon meat,
cut into strips
1 small onion, skinned and
thinly sliced
1oz (25gm) butter
1 can condensed mushroom
soup
¼ pint (125ml) milk
4oz (100gm) packet frozen peas

1. Cut potatoes into cubes.
2. Brown the meat and onion in
butter.
3. Add remaining ingredients and
simmer over a low heat for 10
minutes, stirring frequently.
4. Serve at once.

BRAISED LIVER
Serves 4

1lb (½ kilo) liver, cut into
convenient portions
1oz (25gm) flour, seasoned with
salt and pepper
1oz (25gm) dripping
2 rounded tablespoons dried
onions
¼ pint (125ml) cold water
salt and pepper
gravy browning

1. Coat liver in seasoned flour
and quickly fry in melted dripping
until lightly browned on both
sides.
2. Add dried onions and water
and bring to the boil. Cover the
pan and simmer for 15 minutes.
3. Blend remaining flour with a
little water and stir into the pan.
Cook for a further 3–4 minutes.
4. Adjust seasoning and add a
little gravy browning.
5. Serve with creamed potatoes
and a green vegetable.

LIVER AND ONIONS IN A HURRY
Serves 4

4 large onions
1oz (25gm) lard
4 streaky bacon rashers, cut in
small pieces
6oz (150gm) liver
1oz (25gm) flour, seasoned with
salt and pepper
1 medium can condensed
tomato soup

1. Skin and cut onions into slices.
Fry until browned in lard.
2. Add bacon and fry lightly.
3. Dip liver in seasoned flour and
fry lightly on both sides.
4. Add soup and bring to the boil.
If necessary, add a little water to
thin the soup.
5. Bring to the boil and simmer
for a further 10 minutes, until
liver is cooked.
6. Serve hot with green
vegetables and creamed potatoes.

BACON RICE SUPPER
Serves 4

4oz (100gm) boiled long-grain
rice (raw weight)
8oz (200gm) cooked bacon,
diced
1 packet mushroom sauce
½ pint (250ml) milk
1 small can pineapple tidbits,
drained

1. Preheat oven to moderate to
moderately hot, 375 deg F or gas 5
(190 deg C).
2. Place rice in a casserole dish
and arrange bacon over it.
3. Make up the mushroom sauce
as directed on the packet with
milk and pour over bacon and
rice.
4. Garnish with pineapple and
bake for 20 minutes on centre
shelf.

LEEK AND HAM PIE
Serves 4

1½lb (¾ kilo) potatoes, peeled
2 large leeks, washed and
halved
salt and pepper
8oz (200gm) ham, chopped
1 can chicken soup

1. Preheat oven to hot, 425 deg F
or gas 7 (220 deg C).
2. Parboil potatoes and leeks in
salted water for about 15 minutes.
3. Drain, cut into slices about
¼ inch thick and place in a pie
dish.
4. Sprinkle with salt and pepper
and add chopped ham.
5. Pour soup over and bake in
centre of oven for 20 minutes.

HAM AND SPAGHETTI
Serves 4

8oz (200gm) spaghetti
1½oz (37gm) butter
1 onion, chopped
1 packet mushroom sauce mix
½ pint (250ml) milk
1 small can tomatoes
12oz (300gm) cooked ham, diced
½ level teaspoon dried
marjoram
dash Worcestershire sauce

1. Cook spaghetti in boiling,
salted water. Drain and keep hot.
2. Melt butter in a pan and fry
onion until tender.
3. Stir in the sauce mix and milk
and simmer for 2 minutes.
4. Stir in tomatoes, ham,
marjoram and Worcestershire
sauce. Bring to the boil and
simmer for 15 minutes.
5. Pour sauce over spaghetti.

HAM AND SWEETCORN OMELETTE
Serves 2

4 eggs
1 tablespoon water
salt and pepper
1 packet mushroom sauce mix
½ pint (250ml) milk
1 small can sweetcorn
4oz (100gm) cooked ham, diced
1oz (25gm) butter

1. Break eggs into a basin.
2. Add water, salt and pepper and
mix lightly with a fork.
3. Make up mushroom sauce as
directed on the packet with milk.
4. Add sweetcorn and ham. Keep
hot.
5. Heat butter in an omelette pan.
Pour in the egg mixture and cook
rapidly.
6. Loosen the cooked mixture
around the sides and allow the
liquid to run underneath until the
whole is set.
7. Spoon filling on to one half of
the omelette. Fold second half
over and serve at once, cut into
two portions.

POTATO AND CHICKEN CHOWDER
Serves 4

4 cooked chicken joints
1 can condensed mushroom
soup
1 can (7oz or 175gm) sweetcorn
1 can (19oz or 475gm) new
potatoes
1 tomato, chopped
few drops of Tabasco sauce
salt and pepper
2oz (50gm) double cream

1. Put chicken, soup, sweetcorn,
potatoes, tomato and Tabasco in a
saucepan. Season well.
2. Bring to the boil and simmer
for 15 minutes.
3. When cooked, stir in the cream
and serve with garden peas.

SAUCED CHICKEN
Serves 4

2oz (50gm) butter
1½oz (37gm) flour
½ pint (250ml) milk
¼ pint (125ml) chicken stock
salt and pepper
8oz (200gm) cooked chicken,
chopped
4oz (100gm) mushrooms, lightly
fried
chopped parsley

1. Melt butter in a pan and stir in
the flour.
2. Add milk and stock and stir
until sauce boils.
3. Mix in salt, pepper, chicken
and sliced mushrooms.
4. Heat through and sprinkle
with parsley.

SCRAMBLED CHICKEN
Serves 3–4

2 eggs
4 tablespoons milk
salt and pepper
4oz (100gm) cooked chicken
1 rounded tablespoon
breadcrumbs
½oz (12gm) butter
4 slices hot, buttered toast

1. Mix eggs, milk and seasoning
together.
2. Stir in the chicken and
breadcrumbs.
3. Melt butter in a pan and pour
in the egg mixture. Stir carefully
until cooked.
4. Serve on hot, buttered toast.

CHICKEN A LA KING
Serves 2

1 small onion, chopped
1 small green pepper, chopped
2oz (50gm) butter
1 can condensed cream of
mushroom soup
2–3 tablespoons milk
4oz (100gm) cooked chicken,
cut into small pieces
dash of pepper
fingers of wholemeal bread

1. Cook onion and pepper in
butter until tender.
2. Add soup and milk and mix
well.
3. Add chicken and pepper.
4. Heat, stirring, and serve hot
with fingers of bread.

CHICKEN AND PINEAPPLE
RISSOLES
Serves 4

8oz (200gm) mashed potatoes
8oz (200gm) cooked chicken,
chopped
1 egg
2oz (50gm) brown breadcrumbs
1 small can pineapple rings

1. Mix potatoes and chicken with
a little beaten egg and form into
cakes.
2. Coat with remaining egg and
breadcrumbs and fry in shallow
fat for about 5 minutes on each
side. Drain on kitchen paper.
3. Grill pineapple on both sides,
place one ring on each cake and
serve.

COUNTRY PIE
Serves 4

1 large white loaf
5oz (125gm) butter
12oz (300gm) mushrooms
1 onion
1oz (25gm) flour
½ pint (250ml) milk
salt and pepper
juice of half a lemon
12oz (300gm) cooked chicken
4oz (100gm) ham

1. Preheat oven to moderate, 350
deg F or gas 4 (180 deg C).
2. Remove crust from top of loaf.
Scoop out all the inside, leaving
and empty case.
3. Butter the inside of the case
with 1oz (25gm) butter and put
into oven for about 10 minutes.
4. Heat 2oz (50gm) butter in a pan
and fry mushrooms in it for about
3 minutes.
5. In another pan, heat remaining
butter, add finely sliced onion and
cook gently until onion is tender.
6. Stir in the flour and cook for 2
minutes. Remove pan from heat
and add the milk. Season and
bring to the boil.
7. Add lemon juice and simmer for
at least 3 minutes.
8. Stir in chopped chicken and
ham, then add mushrooms.
9. Fill hot bread case with the
mixture and place top of loaf back
in position.
10. Return loaf to oven for about
5 minutes, then serve with a crisp
green salad.

CHICKEN CHOWDER
Serves 4

A filling soup for a cold night.

¼ pint (125ml) milk
1 pint (approximately ½ litre)
chicken stock
8oz (200gm) potato, peeled and
diced
1 large carrot, diced
1 stick celery, chopped
salt and pepper
1 can sweetcorn
6oz (150gm) cooked chicken,
diced

1. Add milk to stock and bring to
the boil in a saucepan.
2. Add potatoes, carrot, celery,
salt and pepper. Cook for 15
minutes.
3. Drain sweetcorn and add to
the pan, together with the
chicken.
4. Heat through for a further 5
minutes and serve.

PIQUANT TURKEY LEGS
(Illustrated on page 53)
Serves 4

Turkey legs skinned, slashed with
a sharp knife and the cuts filled
with mustard and seasoning.

4 turkey legs
salt and pepper
½ teaspoon cayenne pepper
1 teaspoon made mustard
1½oz (37gm) butter

1. Skin the turkey legs and slit
them with a sharp knife.
2. Sprinkle with salt, pepper and
cayenne pepper.
3. Spread with mustard and leave
for 2 hours.
4. Grill for about 20–30 minutes
until golden, then top each leg
with a cutlet frill.
5. Serve on a bed of lettuce with
watercress and sliced tomatoes.
Accompany with slices of crusty
French bread.

FISH CAKES IN A HURRY
Serves 4

2 packets parsley sauce mix
½ pint (250ml) milk
1lb (½ kilo) cooked white fish,
flaked
1 large packet instant mashed
potato
2oz (50gm) flour
2 eggs
4oz (100gm) breadcrumbs
fat for frying

1. Make up sauce as directed on
the packet, using milk.
2. Add fish and potato, mix well
and spread on a plate to cool.
3. Divide into 12 pieces and shape
into cakes on a floured board.
4. Coat in beaten egg and
breadcrumbs.
5. Fry for about 5 minutes each
side until golden brown. Drain
and serve.

HOT ROES ON TOAST
Serves 4

6oz (150gm) fresh or 1 medium
can soft herring roes
1oz (25gm) flour
1 level teaspoon curry powder
salt and pepper
1oz (25gm) butter
dash of Worcestershire sauce
squeeze lemon juice
4 slices hot buttered toast
parsley to garnish

1. Separate the herring roes.
2. Sift together flour, curry
powder, salt and pepper and toss
the roes in this.
3. Fry gently in butter for a few
minutes only, on each side.
4. Add Worcestershire sauce and
lemon juice to the pan. Cook for a
further minute, shaking the pan
to flavour the roes.
5. Serve the roes on hot toast,
garnished with parsley.

HADDOCK TOPPER
Serves 4

1½lb (¾ kilo) smoked haddock
6oz (150gm) mushrooms
2oz (50gm) butter
salt and pepper
4 eggs
watercress
2 tomatoes

1. Poach haddock in water until
fish is cooked and flakes easily.
Drain carefully and keep hot.
2. Slice mushrooms and cook in
hot butter until tender. Season
well.
3. Poach the eggs and put the
haddock on to a serving dish.
4. Surround with sliced
mushrooms and put the eggs on
top of the fish.
5. Garnish with sprigs of
watercress and sliced tomato.

HADDOCK AND NOODLE PIE
Serves 4

1 medium finnan haddock or
smoked cod
3oz (75gm) noodles
1oz (25gm) butter or margarine
1oz (25gm) flour
½ pint (250ml) milk
6oz (150gm) Cheddar cheese,
grated
salt and pepper

1. Poach haddock or cod in water
for 10–15 minutes.
2. Remove the skin and bones
and flake the fish.
3. Cook noodles in boiling, salted
water until tender.
4. Melt butter or margarine in a
pan, add flour and cook for 2–3
minutes.
5. Remove pan from heat and
gradually add milk. Bring to the
boil and cook for 2–3 minutes.
6. Add 4oz (100gm) cheese and
season to taste.
7. Arrange noodles and haddock
or cod in alternate layers in a
greased pie dish, cover with
cheese sauce and sprinkle with
remaining cheese.
8. Brown under a hot grill and
serve at once.

SMOKED FISH HASH
Serves 4

1½lb (¾ kilo) smoked haddock or
cod fillet
6 bacon rashers
1½lb (¾ kilo) raw potatoes,
finely diced
2 tablespoons chopped onion
2 tablespoons chopped parsley
pepper
2 tablespoons bacon fat or oil
¼ pint (125ml) water
paprika

1. Remove skin and bones from
fish and flake into pieces.
2. Fry bacon until crisp in a
frying pan, then drain on
absorbent paper.
3. Crumble bacon and combine
with potatoes, onion, parsley,
pepper and fish.
4. Place mixture in hot fat and
pour water over the top.
5. Cover and cook over a
moderate heat for 7 minutes.
Turn the mixture and cook
uncovered for 6–8 minutes longer
or until lightly browned, stirring
occasionally.
6. Serve on a hot serving dish
sprinkled with paprika.

CREAMY CURRIED PRAWNS
Serves 4

½oz (12gm) butter
1 tablespoon chopped onion
½ level teaspoon curry powder
1 small eating apple, chopped
1 carton (5oz or 125gm) natural
yogurt
1 egg yolk
salt and pepper
8oz (200gm) peeled prawns
chopped chives and parsley to
garnish

1. Melt butter in a saucepan and
fry onion until soft.
2. Add curry powder and allow to
cook for a few minutes.
3. Stir in apple and yogurt, then
gradually add egg yolk and season
to taste.
4. Cook over a gentle heat until
mixture thickens.
5. Add prawns and cook for a
further 5 minutes.
6. Sprinkle with chives and
parsley and serve with plain
boiled rice.

SPAGHETTI SAVOURY
Serves 4

1 medium can spaghetti in
tomato sauce
salt and pepper
8 eggs
4 tomatoes
4oz (100gm) Cheddar cheese,
grated

1. Heat spaghetti in a frying pan
and add seasoning.
2. Make hollows in spaghetti and
break in the eggs.
3. Cook over a gentle heat for
about 6 minutes.
4. Top with sliced tomatoes and
sprinkle with grated cheese.
5. Grill until golden brown.

QUICK SPAGHETTI BOLOGNESE
Serves 4

1lb ($\frac{1}{2}$ kilo) raw minced beef
1 packet minestrone soup
1 pint (approximately $\frac{1}{2}$ litre)
water

1. Put the beef, contents of
packet of minestone soup and
water into a saucepan and stir
until boiling.
2. Simmer gently for 20 minutes,
stirring occasionally.
3. Serve with hot, boiled
spaghetti.

NOODLES WITH KIDNEY SAUCE
Serves 4

2oz (50gm) butter
1 onion
2 lamb's kidneys
1 small can sweetcorn
1 can kidney soup
10oz (250gm) noodles
$\frac{1}{2}$ teaspoon chopped parsley

1. Melt butter in a pan and fry
chopped onion until transparent.
2. Cut kidney in half, remove skin
and core and cut flesh into small
pieces.
3. Add to pan and fry for 5
minutes.
4. Drain sweetcorn and add to
pan with the soup. Bring slowly
to the boil and simmer for 1
minute.
5. Cook noodles in a large pan of
boiling, salted water for about 10
minutes. Drain and arrange on a
hot serving dish.
6. Pour sauce in centre and serve
sprinkled with chopped parsley.

PAN HASHED POTATOES
Serves 4

2 tomatoes, skinned
1lb ($\frac{1}{2}$ kilo) potatoes, mashed
2 lean bacon rashers, cooked
and diced
salt and pepper
slices of tomato and parsley to
garnish

1. Chop tomatoes and mix with
the rest of the ingredients.
2. With floured hands form into a
round and brown on both sides in
a greased frying pan.
3. Cut into wedges, garnish with
tomato slices and parsley, and
serve with poached or fried eggs.

MUSHROOM OMELETTE
Serves 4

3oz (75gm) butter
8oz (200gm) mushrooms,
chopped
8 eggs
salt and pepper

1. Melt half the butter in an
omelette or frying pan and fry the
mushrooms. Remove from pan.
2. Whisk the eggs, season, and
pour into the hot, buttered pan.
3. Cook until beginning to set,
then add the mushrooms.
4. Cook for a few more minutes,
fold the omelette in half and serve
at once with a salad.

SCANDINAVIAN OMELETTE
Serves 4

1 small onion
1oz (50gm) butter
8oz (200gm) cooked potato,
diced
6 eggs
salt and pepper
$\frac{1}{4}$ level teaspoon mixed herbs
1 can sardines in tomato sauce

1. Chop onion finely.
2. Heat butter in a large omelette
pan or frying pan, add onion and
cook gently without browning,
until tender.
3. Mix in potato. Beat eggs well
with seasoning and herbs.
4. Pour into the pan and increase
the heat.
5. Stir lightly and when eggs are
just set, arrange sardines on top
with tails into the middle.
6. Put pan under a heated grill to
warm the sardines.
7. Serve immediately, in wedges,
with a green salad.

BUTTERED EGGS
Serves 4

4 eggs
4 tablespoons milk
salt and pepper
1oz (25gm) butter
4 slices hot, buttered toast
3 mushrooms
2 tomatoes

1. Beat eggs lightly with milk and seasoning.
2. Melt butter in a pan and add mixture.
3. Stir over a gentle heat until mixture is creamy.
4. Pour it over the toast.
5. Garnish with sliced mushrooms and skinned and sliced tomatoes which have been gently fried in butter.

CHEESE AND EGGS
Serves 4

A pie dish lined with sliced cheese and eggs broken over the top.

2oz (50gm) butter
6oz (150gm) Cheddar cheese
4 eggs
a little chopped parsley
salt and pepper

1. Preheat oven to moderate to moderately hot, 375 deg F or gas 5 (190 deg C).
2. Butter a pie dish and slice in most of the cheese.
3. Break in the eggs and grate remaining cheese over.
4. Top with the rest of the butter and sprinkle with parsley, salt and pepper.
5. Bake for about 10–15 minutes on second shelf down of oven, until eggs are just set.
6. Serve at once.

SUPPER SCRAMBLE
Serves 6

6 slices bread
4oz (100gm) butter
1 teaspoon English mustard
6 thick slices cheese
6 eggs
1 can sweetcorn

1. Toast bread and butter it.
2. Spread with a little mustard.
3. Top each with a slice of cheese.
4. Scramble eggs in butter and stir in the corn.
5. Divide over the toast and serve hot.

CELERY SCRAMBLE
Serves 4

1 can condensed celery soup
8 eggs
4 slices buttered toast

1. Warm undiluted soup in a pan.
2. Beat eggs together lightly and pour into soup. Stir continuously over a low heat until eggs are set.
3. Serve piping hot on buttered toast.

EGG SCRAMBLE
(Illustrated on page 53)
Serves 2

8oz (200gm) cooked chipolata sausages
2oz (50gm) butter
2 thick rounds of bread
1 large eating apple
4 eggs
salt and pepper
2 tablespoons single cream or milk

1. Slice sausages and put into a saucepan with 1oz (25gm) butter.
2. Spread remaining butter over the bread. Toast under a heated grill and keep hot.
3. Peel, core and chop the apple, add to sausages and heat through.
4. Beat eggs well with seasoning and cream or milk.
5. Pour into the pan and stir until just scrambled.
6. Pile eggs on to toast and serve hot with baked beans and green salad.

BACON AND ASPARAGUS OMELETTE
Serves 2

4 streaky bacon rashers
½oz (12gm) dripping
4 eggs
4 tablespoons water
salt and pepper
6 cooked asparagus tips
2oz (50gm) Cheddar cheese, grated
parsley

1. Cut off bacon rinds, chop up bacon and fry in an omelette pan in dripping, until crisp.
2. Remove from pan and keep warm.
3. Pour off all but 1 tablespoon fat.
4. Beat eggs lightly, add water and seasoning; pour into pan when fat is hot.
5. Allow egg mixture to begin to set, then start folding cooked edges to centre.
6. When underside is brown, sprinkle with cooked bacon, fold sides over middle and slide on to a hot, ovenproof plate.
7. Garnish with asparagus tips and cover with grated cheese, then place under a hot grill for a few minutes. Serve immediately.

SUPPER EGGS
Serves 4

1 onion
2oz (50gm) butter
4 tomatoes
4 eggs
salt and pepper
4 slices hot, buttered toast

1. Slice onion finely and fry gently in butter without browning.
2. Skin and chop the tomatoes.
3. Add to the onions and cook until tomatoes are tender.
4. Add beaten eggs and seasoning.
5. Stir lightly until the mixture resembles scrambled eggs.
6. Serve on toast.

EIGHT O'CLOCK SPECIAL
Serves 4

4 bacon rashers
1 tablespoon oil
2 slices white bread
1oz (25gm) butter
1 carton chive-flavoured
cottage cheese
1 eating apple, sliced

1. Dice bacon and fry in oil until crisp and brown. Remove from pan, drain and cool.
2. Remove crusts from bread and cut into ¼-inch cubes.
3. Add butter to frying pan and heat.
4. Fry bread quickly until golden brown and crisp. Drain well on kitchen paper and leave to cool.
5. Mix together cottage cheese, bacon and fried croûtons of bread.
6. Arrange in centre of serving dish.
7. Slice apple over the top and serve.

BACON POTATO PANCAKES
Serves 4

6oz (150gm) streaky bacon
2 large potatoes
1 medium onion
1 egg
1½oz (37gm) self-raising flour
salt and pepper
4oz (100gm) lard

1. Remove rind from bacon and chop finely.
2. Peel potatoes and onion and grate them coarsely into a basin.
3. Add egg, sifted flour and bacon pieces.
4. Season lightly and beat mixture thoroughly with a fork.
5. Heat lard in a frying pan and fry spoonfuls of the mixture until crisp and golden brown on both sides.

BACON OMELETTE
Serves 2–4

6 bacon rashers
8 eggs
2 tablespoons cold water
2 teaspoons chopped parsley
salt and pepper
1oz (25gm) butter

1. Grill or fry the bacon, chop and keep hot.
2. Lightly beat eggs, add water, parsley, salt and pepper.
3. Melt butter in a frying pan and when really hot, but not browned, pour in omelette mixture.
4. Using a fork or palette knife, draw cooked egg from sides to middle of pan. Place bacon in centre.
5. Fold omelette into three and serve at once.

FARMHOUSE SUPPER DISH
(Illustrated on page 53)
Serves 4

3 medium onions
3 sharp eating apples or 1
cooking apple
4 bacon rashers
3oz (75gm) butter
salt and pepper
4 eggs

1. Slice onions and unpeeled apples.
2. Cut up bacon.
3. Heat butter in a large frying pan, and add onion, apple, bacon and seasoning.
4. Cook until onions are tender.
5. Make four hollows in mixture and break eggs in. Cover and leave to cook slowly for a further 3–5 minutes or until eggs are set.

QUICK EGGS FLORENTINE
Serves 4

1 large packet frozen spinach
1oz (25gm) butter
salt and pepper
nutmeg
4 eggs
1 packet cheese sauce mix
½ pint (250ml) milk

1. Cook the spinach as directed on packet and drain well.
2. Chop and add butter, seasoning and a pinch of nutmeg.
3. Place in a fireproof dish.
4. Poach the eggs and arrange on top of spinach. Keep the dish warm.
5. Make up cheese sauce with milk as directed on the packet. Pour over the eggs and spinach.
6. Put under a hot grill for a few minutes, until lightly browned.

SAVOURY EGG SUPPER
Serves 2

4 hard-boiled eggs
1 packet savoury white sauce
mix
½ pint (250ml) milk
1 level desertspoon chopped
parsley
¼ level teaspoon grated nutmeg
2oz (50gm) cheese, grated
1 tablespoon white
breadcrumbs

1. Preheat oven to hot, 425 deg F or gas 7 (220 deg C).
2. Slice the eggs and place in a fireproof dish.
3. Make up white sauce with milk as directed on the packet.
4. Stir in the parsley and nutmeg and pour sauce over eggs.
5. Mix cheese and breadcrumbs together and sprinkle over the dish.
6. Heat through in centre of oven for about 10 minutes.

CHEESE AND EGG TOASTS
Serves 2

6oz (150gm) cheese, grated
1oz (25gm) butter
2 tablespoons milk
salt and pepper
mustard
4 slices white bread
4 eggs

1. Blend the cheese and butter together and mix to a stiff paste with milk.
2. Add salt, pepper and mustard to taste.
3. Toast bread on one side and spread other side with cheese mixture.
4. Cook under a grill until mixture is golden.
5. Meanwhile, poach eggs.
6. Top each slice of toast with a poached egg and serve immediately

FRIED CHEESE AND HAM SANDWICH
Serves 4

8 thin slices white bread, crusts removed
4 slices ham
4 slices Gruyère cheese
2–3oz (50–75gm) butter

1. On four of the bread slices, arrange a slice each of ham and cheese. Top with a second slice of bread.
2. Fry sandwiches in plenty of hot butter. When beginning to brown, turn and fry the second side.
3. Turn several times until both sides are brown and crisp, adding more butter if necessary.
4. Cut in half and serve very hot.

CRAB WITH CHEESE ON TOAST
Serves 4

1 medium can crab meat
2 tablespoons mayonnaise
salt and pepper
8 thin slices white bread
butter for spreading
1 packet processed Cheddar cheese slices

1. Drain and flake the crab meat, removing all bone and sinews.
2. Add mayonnaise, salt and pepper and mix well.
3. Toast the bread slices on both sides and butter while hot.
4. Spread crab mixture evenly on four buttered halves, top with cheese slices and place under a moderately hot grill until cheese is soft and mixture heated through.
5. Top each with remaining toast slices, cut in half and serve.

CHEESE AND CORN RISOTTO
Serves 4

1 onion, chopped
2oz (50gm) butter
6oz (150gm) long-grain rice
1 pint (approximately ½ litre) chicken stock
8oz (200gm) Cheddar cheese
1 can (11oz or 275gm) sweetcorn
8oz (200gm) cooked meat, diced

1. Fry onion in butter and stir in rice.
2. Add stock and simmer for 15–20 minutes.
3. Cut cheese into cubes and add with sweetcorn and meat. Heat through and serve.

FLUFFY CHEESES
Serves 2

4oz (100gm) Cheddar cheese, grated
4 tablespoons milk
2 eggs, separated
4 rounds buttered toast
8 slices tomato

1. Gently heat cheese in milk until melted.
2. Add egg yolks and continue to cook very gently until mixture thickens.
3. Beat egg whites stiffly and fold into mixture.
4. Place rounds of toast in a buttered, ovenware dish.
5. Pour cheese mixture on top and brown lightly under grill.
6. Garnish with tomato slices.

CHEESE TOPPER
Serves 4

1 packet savoury white sauce mix
¼ pint (125ml) milk
8oz (200gm) Lancashire or Cheddar cheese, grated
1 level teaspoon made mustard
1 tablespoon Worcestershire sauce
4 slices of bread
tomato slices and parsley to garnish

1. Make up white sauce as directed on the packet, using only ¼ pint (125ml) milk.
2. Add 6oz (150gm) cheese, mustard and Worcestershire sauce.
3. Heat until cheese has melted, taking care that the mixture does not boil.
4. Meanwhile, make the toast and spread mixture over it.
5. Sprinkle with remaining cheese, brown under a hot grill and serve garnished with tomato slices and parsley.

Summer suppers

Crisp and cold fare for you to enjoy on warm days – colourful salads, meat loaves, savoury jellies and delicious pâtés.

BEEF MAYONNAISE
Serves 4

12oz (300gm) cold beef
2 lettuces
8oz (200gm) tomatoes
4oz (100gm) cucumber
radishes
2 egg yolks
salt and pepper
about ½ pint (250ml) olive oil
juice of half a lemon
2 hard-boiled eggs

1. Cut meat into small dice.
2. Line a salad bowl with the larger lettuce leaves.
3. Cut the firm hearts into quarters and place these at intervals round the sides.
4. Put the meat, skinned and sliced tomatoes, sliced cucumber and radishes into a bowl.
5. Put the egg yolks into a bowl with salt and pepper. Mix with a wooden spoon and then gradually stir in the oil, drop by drop.
6. Add lemon juice at intervals. The mayonnaise should be thick and creamy when ready.
7. Pile the meat mixture and mayonnaise on the lettuce and garnish the dish with sliced hard-boild egg.

BEEF AND BACON SHAPE
Serves 4

6oz (150gm) braising steak
3oz (75gm) bacon
6oz (150gm) sausagemeat
3oz (75gm) breadcrumbs
½ teaspoon chopped parsley
salt and pepper
½ teaspoon dried thyme
1 egg, beaten

1. Put steak, bacon and sausagemeat through the mincer, or chop finely.
2. Blend in breadcrumbs and parsley, season well and add thyme. Bind with egg.
3. Press mixture into a greased loaf tin, wrap in a cloth and steam or boil for 2 hours.
4. Serve cold with salad.

ALL-IN-ONE-SALAD
Serves 4

12oz (300gm) cooked meat, diced
6oz (150gm) cold, boiled long-grain rice (raw weight)
1 packet (8oz or 200gm) frozen, mixed vegetables, cooked and left to cool
12 tablespoons mayonnaise
salt and pepper
lettuce or white cabbage leaves
tomato wedges and slices of green pepper to garnish

1. Toss all ingredients together, except for the lettuce or cabbage and garnish. Chill.
2. Serve on fresh lettuce or white cabbage leaves and garnish with tomato and green pepper.

SALAMI AND CHEESE CORNETS
(Illustrated on page 54)
Serves 4

3oz (75gm) cheese, grated
1 tablespoon chutney
2 tablespoons crushed potato crisps
4oz (100gm) sliced salami, pork sausage or ham sausage
a few cloves
stuffed olives and lettuce leaves to garnish

1. Mix together cheese, chutney and crushed crisps.
2. Make a cut from the centre to the edge of each round of meat.
3. Overlap the two cut edges to form a cornet and secure with a clove.
4. Fill with cheese mixture and top with slices of stuffed olive.
5. Serve on a bed of lettuce.

PATE OF PORK
Serves 4

4oz (100gm) streaky bacon rashers
4oz (100gm) pig's liver
12oz (300gm) lean pork
4oz (100gm) salt belly of pork
½ small onion, chopped
2oz (50gm) white breadcrumbs
salt
pinch of ground mace
black pepper
½ teaspoon chopped rosemary
1 small egg
1oz (25gm) butter, melted

1. Preheat oven to very moderate, 325 deg F or gas 3 (170 deg C).
2. Line a small buttered casserole with bacon.
3. Mince meats with onion several times.
4. Add breadcrumbs, salt, mace, pepper, rosemary and egg.
5. Mix in a little water to give a dropping consistency, then turn into the bacon-lined dish.
6. Cover with buttered paper and a lid and set casserole in a roasting tin of cold water.
7. Cook in centre of oven for 3½ hours.
8. Remove lid, replace paper and press under a weight until cold.
9. Pour remaining butter over and serve, sliced, with salad.

PORK CHEESE
Serves 4

1lb (½ kilo) cold roast pork
4oz (100gm) pork fat
salt and pepper
2 teaspoons chopped parsley
4 sage leaves, chopped
2 blades of mace, powdered
a little grated nutmeg
1 teaspoon finely grated lemon rind
some good gravy or stock

1. Preheat oven to moderately hot, 400 deg F or gas 6 (200 deg C).
2. Cut cold pork and fat into small, even-sized pieces.
3. Season well and add parsley, sage, mace, nutmeg and lemon rind.
4. Mix all the ingredients thoroughly and put into a greased mould or basin.
5. Fill up with gravy or stock, cover and bake in centre of oven for 1 hour.
6. When cold, serve with salad.

LIVER PATE
(Illustrated on page 54)
Serves 4

12oz (300gm) pig's liver
8oz (200gm) fat pork
½ pint (250ml) milk
2oz (50gm) plain flour
1 teaspoon allspice
3 tablespoons dry sherry (optional)
salt and pepper
2oz (50gm) butter, melted

1. Preheat oven to very moderate, 325 deg F or gas 3 (170 deg C).
2. Mince liver and pork together three or four times.
3. Blend in milk, flour, allspice and sherry.
4. Stir in seasoning and butter.
5. Turn into a buttered dish and put the dish in a roasting tin of cold water.
6. Cover with foil and bake in centre of oven for about 1 hour, or until firm.
7. Leave to get quite cold and garnish with watercress. Serve with lettuce, tomato and cucumber slices and fingers of toast with butter.

LIVER SHAPE
Serves 4

1lb (½ kilo) pig's liver
4oz (100gm) belly of pork
3oz (75gm) oatmeal or porridge oats
1oz (25gm) suet
½ teaspoon basil
1 teaspoon ginger
salt and pepper

1. Mince all ingredients together twice, using a fine mincer.
2. Grease a 1-pint (approximately ½ litre) basin and press the mixture in.
3. Cover and steam for 1½ hours.
4. Serve hot or cold, garnished with watercress.

HAM WITH PIQUANT RICE
Serves 4

1 can (1lb or ½ kilo) ham
2oz (50gm) butter
5oz (150gm) boiled long-grain rice (raw weight)
salt
1 teaspoon prepared mustard
1 garlic clove, crushed
2–3 tablespoons French dressing (see Basic recipes, page 100)
1 tablespoon tomato ketchup

1. Slice ham downwards into eight slices and fry in butter.
2. Mix rice with salt and mustard.
3. Add garlic and French dressing and stir in tomato ketchup.
4. Serve with the hot fried ham.

SAVOURY LOAF
Serves 4

1lb (½ kilo) sausages
2 bacon rashers
1 tablespoon chopped parsley
¼ teaspoon mixed herbs
2 teaspoons chopped onion
salt and pepper
1 tablespoon stock
4 tablespoons browned crumbs
2 tablespoons finely chopped celery

1. Skin the sausages and mince the bacon.
2. Mix with parsley, herbs, onion and seasoning.
3. Moisten with stock and form into a roll. Tie in a floured cloth and boil for 1 hour.
4. When cool, roll it in browned crumbs.
5. Garnish with celery and serve on a bed of salad.

VEAL AND GAMMON LOAF
Serves 4–6

2oz (50gm) butter
8oz (200gm) veal, minced
6oz (150gm) gammon, chopped
1 large onion, chopped
1 garlic clove, crushed
3oz (75gm) white breadcrumbs
1 egg
few drops of Worcestershire sauce
pinch of mixed herbs
salt and pepper

1. Preheat oven to moderate to moderately hot, 375 deg F or gas 5 (190 deg C).
2. Heat butter in a large frying pan and gently fry veal, gammon, onion and garlic for 5 minutes.
3. Mix fried mixture with breadcrumbs, egg, Worcestershire sauce, mixed herbs, salt and pepper.
4. Place mixture in a well greased 1-lb (½ kilo) loaf tin. Cover securely with foil or greaseproof paper.
5. Stand tin in a roasting tin half filled with boiling water and bake in centre of oven for 1 hour.
6. Remove cover and replace with fresh greaseproof paper. Press with a heavy weight and leave until quite cold.
7. Turn out the meat loaf and serve sliced with a salad.

CHICKEN SALAD CAPRICE
Serves 4

1 large ripe banana
2 tablespoons lemon juice
1 large orange
12oz (300gm) cooked chicken
3 tablespoons mayonnaise
2 tablespoons cream
crisp lettuce leaves
4oz (100gm) black grapes

1. Slice the banana into a bowl and toss in lemon juice.
2. Peel the orange and divide into segments. Remove skin and pips and add segments to the bowl.
3. Add chicken cut into ½-inch dice, mayonnaise and cream.
4. Mix lightly and set aside in a cool place for 1 hour.
5. Line a shallow bowl with lettuce leaves, pile chicken mixture in the centre and garnish with halved and de-seeded grapes.

CHICKEN AND HAM JELLY
Serves 4

1 pint (approximately ½ litre) aspic jelly (see Basic recipes, page 100)
1 can asparagus
1 small can sliced carrots
12oz (300gm) cooked chicken
8oz (200gm) cooked ham

1. Set a layer of jelly in a mould.
2. Dip some asparagus tips in the liquid aspic jelly and set them in a pattern in the mould.
3. Cover with another thin layer of liquid jelly and leave to set until firm.
4. Mix together carrots, chopped chicken and ham and the remaining asparagus, chopped. Pour remaining jelly over and mix well.
5. When beginning to set, pour mixture into the mould and leave to set.
6. Turn out and serve with a salad.

CHICKEN SALAD WITH SWEETCORN
Serves 4

8oz (200gm) long-grain rice
¼ pint (125ml) mayonnaise
½ teaspoon paprika
1 small can garden oeas
1 small can sweetcorn
1 red pepper, diced
1 green pepper, diced
2 tablespoons sliced spring onions
12oz (300gm) cooked chicken, sliced
salt and pepper

1. Cook rice in plenty of boiling, salted water for about 15 minutes, or until tender.
2. Drain well, fork through and leave to cool.
3. Pour mayonnaise into a salad bowl and add paprika, peas, sweetcorn, red and green peppers, spring onions and chicken.
4. Mix well together, check seasoning and gently add cold rice to the mixture.
5. Serve immediately.

CHICKEN AND CUCUMBER SALAD
Serves 4

1 large cucumber
2 tablespoons thin cream
2 tablespoons mayonnaise
2 teaspoons lemon juice
1 teaspoon finely chopped fresh mint
shake of salt
12oz (300gm) cooked chicken meat
2 firm tomatoes, sliced
1 hard-boiled egg, sliced

1. Cut cucumber in half, thinly slice one half and cut the other half into very small cubes.
2. Prepare dressing by mixing cream, mayonnaise, lemon juice, mint and salt together, then stir in the cubes of cucumber and chopped chicken.
3. Set aside in a cool place for 1 hour for the flavours to blend.
4. When ready to serve, pile chicken mixture in the centre of a flat dish, circle with cucumber slices and garnish with tomato and egg slices.

MOUSSE OF CHICKEN
Serves 4

½oz (12gm) gelatine
¼ pint (125ml) chicken stock
8oz (200gm) cooked chicken, minced
¼ pint (125ml) mayonnaise
juice of half a lemon
salt and pepper
¼ pint (125ml) double cream, lightly whipped

1. Dissolve the gelatine in stock over a low heat.
2. Stir in minced chicken.
3. Add mayonnaise, lemon juice, salt and pepper.
4. Blend in the cream, turn into a mould and leave to set.
5. Turn out to serve with salad.

RICE AND CHICKEN SALAD
Serves 4

6oz (150gm) long-grain rice
1 garlic clove (optional)
3 tablespoons corn oil
1 tablespoon wine or tarragon vinegar
salt and pepper
2 level tablespoons seedless raisins
1 green pepper, finely sliced
2 tomatoes, peeled and chopped
12oz (300gm) cooked chicken, diced

1. Cook rice in boiling, salted water for 10–15 minutes, until tender. Drain well.
2. Rub a salad bowl with cut garlic, if liked.
3. Mix corn oil, vinegar, salt and pepper with a fork in the salad bowl.
4. Add hot rice and raisins and toss in dressing.
5. Stir the pepper, tomato and chicken into the rice. Allow to cool before serving.

HERRING AND APPLE SALAD
Serves 4

1 small jar pickled herrings
1 large cooking apple
1 small carton soured cream
dash of Tabasco sauce
1 lettuce

1. Strain herrings and cut into small pieces. Put into a bowl.
2. Peel, core and chop the apple and add to herring.
3. Stir in soured cream and Tabasco.
4. Arrange lettuce on a dish and serve the salad in the centre.

BEER-SOUSED HERRINGS
Serves 4

4 large herrings
2 bayleaves
1 large onion
1 small can brown ale
1 teaspoon sugar
½ teaspoon salt

1. Preheat oven to cool, 300 deg F or gas 2 (150 deg C).
2. Wash and bone herrings and roll up each one. Arrange in a heatproof dish with bayleaves.
3. Slice onion and arrange over the herrings. Pour beer over and sprinkle with sugar and salt.
4. Cover dish with foil and bake in centre of oven for about 1 hour.
5. Leave to cool and drain off beer before serving with a green salad.

SOUSED MACKEREL
Serves 4

4 mackerel
1 large onion
1 blade of mace
12 peppercorns
4 cloves
1 bayleaf
vinegar and water

1. Preheat oven to moderate, 350 deg F or gas 4 (180 deg C).
2. Clean the mackerel and cut off heads and tails.
3. Slice onion and put it in a fireproof dish with mackerel and herbs.
4. Cover with equal quantities of vinegar and water.
5. Cover with greaseproof paper and cook in centre of oven for 1–1½ hours.
6. Leave to cool in the liquid.
7. Serve with salad.

SMOKED TROUT MOUSSE
Serves 4

2 smoked trout, skinned and boned
1oz (25gm) butter, softened
juice of half a lemon
salt, pepper and a pinch of cayenne
½ pint (250ml) double cream, whipped
lemon and cucumber slices to garnish

1. Pound trout using pestle and mortar or a wooden spoon.
2. Add softened butter and lemon juice. Mix well and season to taste.
3. Gently fold in cream.
4. Turn into four individual dishes and chill.
5. Garnish with lemon and cucumber slices.

TOMATO AND FISH SALAD
Serves 4

¾oz (18gm) gelantine
3 teaspoons sugar
2 teaspoons piquant table sauce
salt and pepper
1½ pints (approximately ¾ litre) tomato juice
2oz (50gm) cooked peas
1½lb (¾ kilo) cooked white fish
¼ pint (125ml) white sauce (see Basic recipes, page 100)
chopped chives, shrimps and watercress to garnish

1. Dissolve gelatine in a little hot water.
2. Mix sugar, piquant sauce, salt, pepper and tomato juice and add gelatine.
3. Pour a little of this mixture into a damp ring mould.
4. Add peas, then the rest of the liquid and allow to set.
5. Turn out on to a dish and fill centre of mould with the fish, bound together with white sauce.
6. Garnish with chopped chives, shrimps and watercress.

HADDOCK MOUSSE
Serves 8

2lb (1 kilo) fresh haddock
¾ pint (375ml) milk
1½oz (37gm) butter
1½oz (37gm) flour
1oz (12gm) gelatine, dissolved in a little hot water
grated rind and juice of 1 lemon
salt, pepper and cayenne pepper
½ pint (250ml) double cream
cucumber slices

1. Poach haddock in milk. When cool drain off and reserve the milk, and flake fish.
2. Make a sauce by melting the butter in a pan and adding flour. Remove from heat and gradually add the milk in which fish was poached, stirring constantly.
3. Cook for 1 minute till smooth and glossy. Leave to cool.
4. Add flaked fish, gelatine, lemon rind and juice. Season well.
5. Whip cream and fold into the mixture.
6. Tie a band of paper round a 1-pint (approximately ½ litre) soufflé dish and butter lightly.
7. Pour mixture into soufflé dish and leave to set.
8. Remove band of paper before serving and garnish with slices of cucumber.

ANCHOVY SALAD
Serves 4

¼ small cabbage, finely shredded
4 tablespoons bottled French dressing (or see Basic recipes, page 100)
6 anchovies
4oz (100gm) cooked potato, diced
1 tablespoon chopped onion
1 tablespoon chopped gherkin
¼ pint (125ml) salad dressing
watercress to garnish

1. Toss cabbage in French dressing and arrange on a dish.
2. Bone anchovies and chop them.
3. Mix with potato, onion and gherkin and add salad dressing.
4. Pile on the cabbage and garnish with watercress.

Pork chops tropicale (see page 77) French beef with creamed potatoes (see page 75)

Gammon supper with green salad (see page 80) · Cider chicken and sweetcorn (see page 82)

Chocolate mousse (see page 93)   Flan aux pommes (see page 96)

Crunchy lemon pie with cream (see page 86)   Sherry-baked bananas (see page 98)

SHRIMP PLATTER
Serves 4

4 tomatoes
1 small can shrimps
4 eggs
¼ pint (250ml) white sauce (see Basic recipes, page 100)
3oz (75gm) cheese, grated
watercress to garnish

1. Preheat oven to hot, 425 deg F or gas 7 (220 deg C).
2. Skin and slice tomatoes.
3. Drain shrimps.
4. Arrange tomatoes in a shallow, ovenware dish. Cover with shrimps, reserving a few for garnish.
5. Poach eggs and arrange over the shrimps.
6. Make white sauce and add cheese, stirring well.
7. Coat the eggs with the sauce and place the dish in oven for 5–10 minutes until browned.
8. Garnish with watercress sprigs and remaining shrimps.

VICHYSSOISE
Serves 4

A chilled leek and potato soup.

1lb (½ kilo) leeks
1 medium onion
1oz (25gm) butter
3 medium potatoes, washed, peeled and quartered
1½ pints (approximately ¾ litre) chicken stock
salt and pepper
¼ pint (125ml) single cream
chopped chives to garnish

1. Cut off most of the green part of the leeks and make cuts down the stem, without cutting into the bulbous part.
2. Wash thoroughly under cold running water, then slice thinly.
3. Chop onion finely.
4. Melt butter in a saucepan, add leeks and onion and fry gently for 10 minutes with lid on pan.
5. Add potatoes and stock and simmer for about 30 minutes in a covered pan, until soft. Season to taste.
6. Rub through a sieve or put in a blender.
7. Pour into a soup tureen and stir in the cream.
8. Adjust seasoning and chill.
9. Garnish with chives just before serving.

APPLE SALADS
(Illustrated on page 54)
Serves 4

Eating apples hollowed out and filled with a mixture of cheese, walnuts and celery.

4 large eating apples
2oz (50gm) cheese, finely grated
1½oz (37gm) walnuts, chopped
¼ head celery, chopped
¼ pint (125ml) cream, lightly whipped
juice of 1 lemon
4 walnuts

1. Wash and cut a slice off top of apples and scoop out the insides.
2. Discard cores and chop rest of apple that has been scooped out.
3. Mix with cheese, nuts and celery and fold gently into cream.
4. Pile back into the apple shells which have been sprinkled with a little lemon juice.
5. Top with a walnut and serve chilled.

JELLIED TOMATOES
(Illustrated on page 54)
Serves 4

1oz (25gm) gelatine
½ pint (250ml) stock
4 large tomatoes
1 cooked carrot, diced
3oz (75gm) cooked veal or chicken, shredded

1. Dissolve gelatine in stock over heat.
2. Cut tomatoes in half, scoop out pulp and sieve into stock. Add carrot and meat.
3. When jelly is nearly set, chill and spoon into tomato shells.
4. Leave to set firmly and serve with a green salad.

TOMATO CUPS
Serves 4

Hollowed-out tomatoes filled with cottage cheese and cream.

4 large tomatoes
4 tablespoons cream
1 small carton cottage cheese
shake of paprika
½ small cucumber
1 lettuce
3 crispy bacon rashers, fried

1. Slice the tops off the tomatoes and scoop out the insides.
2. Gently mix cream into cottage cheese and spoon into tomatoes.
3. Sprinkle the tops with paprika pepper.
4. Thinly peel and slice the cucumber.
5. Arrange the tomatoes on a bed of lettuce garnished with cucumber and chopped bacon rashers.

TOMATO SALAD MOULD
Serves 4

3oz (75gm) Cheddar cheese
1½lb (¾ kilo) tomatoes, sieved
salt and pepper
1 rounded teaspoon gelatine
2oz (50gm) cooked green peas
2oz (50gm) mushrooms, cooked and chopped

1. Grate cheese and add to tomatoes in a bowl. Season well.
2. Dissolve gelatine in 2 tablespoons hot water, stir into the tomato mixture with peas and mushrooms.
3. Turn into a mould and leave to set.
4. Turn out to serve with a green salad.

JELLIED EGGS
Serves 6

6 lightly poached eggs, or
hard-boiled eggs, shelled
1 can condensed consommé
lettuce
sliced stuffed olives to garnish

1. Drain the poached eggs and
place in individual dishes, or cut
hard-boiled eggs in half.
2. Heat consommé gently in a
small pan, then allow to cool.
3. Cover eggs with consommé and
place in refrigerator.
4. Serve chilled with lettuce and
garnished with sliced olives.

MAYONNAISE SALAD EGGS
Serves 4

4 eggs
3 tablespoons cream
1 tomato, skinned and sieved
1oz (25gm) cheese, finely grated
salt and pepper
1 lettuce
¼ pint (125ml) mayonnaise

1. Hard boil the eggs and shell
them.
2. Trim a slice from the tops of
the eggs so they will stand
upright.
3. Cut a lid off each egg, scoop
out the yolks and sieve them into
a bowl.
4. Add cream, tomato, cheese and
seasoning.
5. Pile mixture back into the eggs,
stand them on a bed of lettuce and
replace lids. Spoon mayonnaise
over and serve.

EGG BUTTERFLIES
Serves 4

4 large, firm tomatoes
2 hard-boiled eggs
4 slices brown bread, buttered
a little mustard and cress

1. Wipe the tomatoes and place
them stem side down.
2. With a sharp knife cut the
tomato almost in half and then in
half again.
3. Slice the eggs thinly and put a
slice very carefully between the
tomato quarters.
4. Put each tomato on a slice of
brown bread and garnish with
mustard and cress.

CHEESE AND CELERY SALAD
Serves 4

4oz (100gm) cream cheese
2 tablespoons chopped celery
2 tablespoons chopped apple
1 teaspoon chopped parsley
celery sticks to garnish

1. Mix cheese, celery, apple and
parsley together.
2. Arrange in a dish with sticks
of celery at each side.

CHEESE AND CABBAGE SALAD
Serves 4

½ small white cabbage (about
12oz or 300gm), shredded
2 sticks celery, thinly sliced
1 small onion, finely chopped
8oz (200gm) Cheddar cheese,
grated
3 tablespoons salad cream
3 tablespoons olive oil
1½ tablespoons white vinegar
salt and pepper
watercress to garnish

1. Mix together cabbage, celery,
onion and 6oz (150gm) cheese.
2. Beat together salad cream,
olive oil, vinegar and seasoning.
3. Add this dressing to cabbage
mixture and mix well.
4. Arrange in a serving dish and
sprinkle remaining cheese on top.
5. Garnish with watercress and
serve.

COTTAGE CHEESE AND MUSHROOM SALAD
Serves 4

4 tablespoons salad oil
4 tablespoons white vinegar
1 teaspoon sugar
salt and pepper
1 teaspoon French mustard
1 large onion, finely chopped
8 large open mushrooms
1 lettuce
½ cucumber, sliced
8oz (200gm) cottage cheese

1. Beat together oil, vinegar,
sugar, salt, pepper and mustard.
Alternatively, put these
ingredients into a screw-topped
jar and shake vigorously.
2. Add onion.
3. Wash mushrooms, remove the
stalks and place the heads in a
bowl.
4. Pour dressing over and leave
to soak for a few hours.
5. Arrange lettuce leaves and
cucumber slices in four individual
serving dishes.
6. Place mushrooms on salad and
top each with a spoonful of
cottage cheese.

SWISS CHEESE BOATS
Serves 4–6

6 bridge rolls
2 tablespoons salad cream
1 can (7½oz or 187gm) tuna
6 Swiss processed cheese
triangles
3oz (75gm) butter

1. Slice tops off rolls, scoop out
the insides and crumble the bread.
2. Spread salad cream into each
hollowed-out roll.
3. Blend tuna with breadcrumbs
and pile into rolls. Top with
halved Swiss processed cheese
triangles and replace lids.
4. Sieve rest of Swiss processed
cheese triangles into a basin and
beat with butter until smooth.
5. Pipe this mixture round the
edges of the lids.
6. Serve with a crisp green salad.

Friends coming in for the evening? I have chosen a selection of recipes that should please any gourmet guest.

FRENCH BEEF
(Illustrated on page 71)
Serves 6

2oz (50gm) dripping
1 carrot, peeled and sliced
2 onions, sliced
2lb (1 kilo) topside or round
of beef, cut into dice
2oz (50gm) flour
½ pint (250ml) red wine
½ pint (250ml) beef stock
bouquet garni
20 button mushrooms

1. Melt the dripping in a heavy pan.
2. Add carrot and onions and fry gently for a few minutes.
3. Remove, and brown the meat on all sides. Remove meat and stir in the flour.
5. Add wine, stock, bouquet garni and stir until sauce is smooth.
6. Return meat, vegetables and add button mushrooms to the pan.
7. Cover with greased paper and simmer gently for 3 hours.
8. Serve with creamed potatoes.

BEEF STROGANOFF
Serves 4

2oz (50gm) butter
2 tablespoons oil
1½lb (¾ kilo) tender beef fillet,
cut into thin strips
1 medium onion, finely chopped
4oz (100gm) button mushrooms,
sliced
¼ pint (125ml) white wine
2 teaspoons tomato purée
dash of Worcestershire sauce
2 cartons (5oz or 125gm each)
soured cream
salt and freshly ground pepper
chopped parsley

1. Melt butter in a strong frying pan or flameproof casserole and add 1 tablespoon oil to prevent butter from browning.
2. Fry beef strips in hot fat for about 1 minute, browning on all sides.
3. Remove meat from pan and add remaining oil to pan.
4. Add onion and cook for 2–3 minutes.
5. Add mushrooms and continue cooking for 1–2 minutes.
6. Pour in wine, tomato purée and Worcestershire sauce and boil rapidly for about 2 minutes.
7. Return meat to pan, reduce heat and stir in soured cream. Do not boil it.
8. Stir until well blended and heated through. Season to taste.
9. Garnish with parsley and serve with plain, boiled rice or creamed potatoes.

BEEF OLIVES
Serves 4–6

1 packet onion and mushroom
stuffing
1½lb (¾ kilo) shoulder beef,
sliced and trimmed
1oz (25gm) butter
1 onion, finely chopped
1 pint (approximately ½ litre)
stock
salt and pepper
parsley sprigs to garnish

1. Prepare stuffing according to directions on the packet.
2. Flatten meat with a wooden rolling pin and cut into rectangles 2 inches by 3 inches.
3. Place 1 teaspoon stuffing on each piece of meat, roll up and tie with fine string.
4. Melt butter in a saucepan and fry onion until golden.
5. Add beef olives and fry until browned.
6. Add stock, salt and pepper.
7. Cover and simmer for approximately 1 hour 20 minutes, until tender.
8. Remove string from olives, place on a hot dish and pour gravy over.
9. Garnish with parsley sprigs.

FESTIVE BEEF
Serves 4

1lb (½ kilo) stewing steak, diced
1oz (25gm) lard
½oz (12gm) flour
½ pint (250ml) red wine
¼ pint (125ml) water
1 garlic clove, crushed
(optional)
2 teaspoons tomato purée
salt and pepper
3oz (75gm) lean bacon,
de-rinded and cut into strips
12 baby onions, peeled
4oz (200gm) mushrooms,
peeled and quartered

1. Brown meat on all sides in hot
lard in a saucepan for 2–3
minutes.
2. Sprinkle in the flour and brown
it carefully.
3. Add wine, water, garlic,
tomato purée, salt and pepper.
4. Fry bacon and onions together
in a pan for 5 minutes, then add
to the meat.
5. Cover with wetted greaseproof
paper and a lid and simmer gently
for 1½ hours.
6. Add mushrooms and cook for a
further 10–15 minutes.

TOMATO-BAKED STEAK
Serves 4

Easy to prepare and yet
glamorous enough for special
guests.

1lb (½ kilo) fillet steak
2oz (50gm) butter
3 tomatoes
1 onion
salt and pepper
¼ pint (125ml) cream
2 tablespoons water

1. Preheat oven to moderately
hot, 400 deg F or gas 6 (200 deg C).
2. Beat steak with a heavy knife
and brown the outside gently in
butter, without cooking the meat.
3. Lay the steak in a casserole
and add sliced tomatoes and
onions. Season well.
4. Pour cream and water over,
cover very closely with foil and
cook in centre of oven for 30
minutes.

ONION-TOPPED STEAK
Serves 4

1½lb (¾ kilo) rump steak
salt and pepper
2oz (50gm) lard
4 large onions
1oz (25gm) flour
½ pint (250ml) water or stock

1. Beat the steak, season well and
fry in lard until just cooked
through on both sides.
2. Remove meat from pan and
keep hot.
3. Slice the onions and fry until
crisp. Add to meat and drain off
most of the fat.
6. Add flour and stir until
browned then blend in water or
stock and cook until thickened.
7. Top steak with onion rings,
season and strain gravy over the
top.

OVEN-BAKED STEAK
Serves 4

1lb (½ kilo) fillet steak
2oz (50gm) butter
salt and pepper
2 large onions
¼ pint (125ml) cream
4 tablespoons beef stock

1. Preheat oven to moderate, 350
deg F or gas 4 (180 deg C).
2. Slice the fillet steak and brown
in butter.
3. Put into a casserole dish and
sprinkle with salt and pepper.
5. Skin and chop onions and
brown in butter then scatter over
the steak.
6. Pour cream and stock over,
cover closely and cook in centre
of oven for 1 hour.

FILLET STEAK FLAMBE
Serves 4

Here's a party piece for a
company occasion.

1½lb (¾ kilo) fillet or rump
steak, cut into 4 pieces.
2 tablespoons olive oil
salt and pepper
2 veal kidneys
3oz (75gm) butter
6oz (150gm) button mushrooms,
sliced
1 can pineapple slices
1 small can cherries, stoned
and drained
1 small can artichoke bottoms
2 tablespoons brandy

1. Brush steak with oil, season
and grill on both sides.
2. Skin the kidneys, slice into fine
shreds and fry in butter in a heavy
frying pan.
3. Add mushrooms and cook until
tender.
4. Mix in drained pineapple slices.
5. Chop and add cherries to
pineapple, reserving 4 whole ones,
and heat through gently.
6. Heat artichoke bottoms
through in their own liquid.
7. Top each steak with a drained
artichoke and a cherry on a
cocktail stick.
8. Arrange steaks in centre of
pan of kidneys, fruits and
vegetables. Heat through gently.
9. Warm the brandy very gently
in a pan, spoon over the meat and
ignite at once.
10. Serve straight to the table in
the pan in which it was cooked.

HUNGARIAN GOULASH
Serves 4

2oz (50gm) fat
1 large onion, sliced
2 garlic cloves, crushed
1½lb (¾ kilo) chuck steak,
trimmed and cut into pieces
4 bacon rashers
8oz (200gm) mushrooms, sliced
6 tomatoes, skinned and sliced
1 green pepper, cut into rings
2–3 dried chillies
1 level tablespoon paprika
¾ level teaspoon caraway seeds
1 bayleaf
¼ teaspoon marjoram
¼ teaspoon thyme
salt and pepper
¼ pint (125ml) soured cream
½ teaspoon chopped parsley

1. Preheat oven to cool, 300 deg F
or gas 2 (150 deg C).
2. Melt fat in a saucepan and
lightly fry onion and garlic.
3. Add meat and bacon and fry
quickly until browned.
4. Add mushrooms, tomatoes,
green pepper, spices and herbs.
Season with salt and pepper and
bring slowly to simmering point.
5. Place in an ovenware casserole
and cook on the second shelf
down from the top of oven for
1½–2 hours.
6. Adjust seasoning if necessary.
7. Add soured cream, garnish
with chopped parsley and serve
immediately.

CURRY OF LAMB
Serves 4

1lb (½ kilo) shoulder of lamb,
boned and cut into pieces
salt and pepper
4 onions, peeled and sliced
2 tablespoons curry powder
1 teaspoon brown sugar
large pinch of ground ginger
1 lemon
2 chicken stock cubes
chopped parsley

1. Sprinkle lamb with salt and
pepper.
2. Fry lamb, onions, curry
powder, sugar and ginger in a
large pan for 5 minutes.
3. Add grated rind and juice of
lemon and stock cubes.
4. Cover with cold water, bring
to the boil, cover and simmer for 2
hours.
5. Sprinkle with parsley and serve
with plain, boiled rice.

PORK AND PINEAPPLE RINGS
Serves 4

4 pork chops
olive oil
salt and pepper
1 can pineapple rings
3 tablespoons white wine
rind of 1 lemon
2 teaspoons arrowroot

1. Brush chops with oil, season
and grill for 10–15 minutes on
each side.
2. Drain pineapple rings and add
enough pineapple juice to wine to
make up to ½ pint (250ml) liquid.
Add lemon rind.
4. Blend arrowroot with a little
pineapple juice and add to liquid.
5. Bring to the boil, stirring until
it thickens, then strain off lemon
rind.
6. Brush pineapple rings with oil
and grill for 1 minute on each
side.
7. Place them on the chops and
pour the wine sauce over.

PORK CHOPS TROPICALE
(Illustrated on page 71)
Serves 4

4 pork chops
1oz (25gm) lard
½ pint (250ml) orange juice
2 tablespoons brown sugar
1 teaspoon powdered ginger
1 teaspoon salt
pepper
¼ teaspoon Tabasco sauce
1 tablespoon cornflour
1 tablespoon water
4 pineapple slices, halved
4 slices orange

1. Preheat oven to moderate, 350
deg F or gas 4 (180 deg C).
2. Brown chops on both sides in
fat, then transfer to a casserole.
3. Mix orange juice with sugar,
ginger, salt, pepper and Tabasco
and pour over the chops.
4. Bake in centre of oven for
about an hour.
5. Place the drained chops on a
hot serving dish and keep warm.
6. Mix cornflour and water with
meat juices and cook until sauce
has boiled and thickened.
7. Garnish chops with pineapple
and orange slices and pour sauce
over.
8. Serve with creamed potatoes.

SAVOURY TOMATO PORK CHOPS
Serves 4

4 pork chops
1 level teaspoon dry mustard
1 level teaspoon caster sugar
1 tablespoon salad oil
1 onion, sliced
1 medium can condensed tomato soup
½ soup can water
1 medium can carrots
4oz (100gm) mushrooms, sliced
juice of half a lemon
1 bayleaf
1 small packet frozen peas

1. Trim the chops and sprinkle with mustard and sugar mixed together.
2. Brown well on both sides in hot oil, then remove from pan.
3. Drain away all but 1 teaspoon oil and add onion. Cook gently until onion is tender and lightly browned.
4. Replace chops in the pan and pour mixed soup and water over.
5. Add the drained and sliced carrots, mushrooms, lemon juice and bayleaf. Cover and simmer gently for 1 hour.
6. Remove bayleaf, add peas and simmer for a further 10 minutes.

GRILLED PORK WITH LEMON
Serves 4

4 sparerib chops
salt and pepper
1 lemon
2 teaspoons chopped, fresh rosemary, or 1 teaspoon dried rosemary
2oz (50gm) butter

1. Wipe and trim the chops and sprinkle with salt and pepper.
2. Grate rind from half the lemon.
3. Sprinkle chops both sides with juice from half the lemon and with half the rosemary.
4. Grill gently for 10–15 minutes on each side until golden brown. Keep hot.
5. Add butter to pan with remaining lemon juice, grated rind and remaining rosemary. Heat through for 2–3 minutes.
6. Arrange chops on a serving dish and pour sauce over.

VEAL WITH HAM POCKETS
Serves 4

4 veal cutlets
4 thin slices cooked ham
1oz (25gm) butter, melted
toasted breadcrumbs
2oz (50gm) Cheddar cheese, grated
½ pint (250ml) white sauce (see Basic recipes, page 100)

1. Preheat oven to moderate, 350 deg F or gas 4 (180 deg C).
2. Cut through each cutlet, from the side to the bone, to make a pocket.
3. Press a folded slice of ham into each cutlet.
4. Brush the cutlets with melted butter and coat in breadcrumbs.
5. Place in an ungreased, fireproof dish and bake in centre of oven for 30 minutes.
6. Stir cheese into white sauce, pour over the veal and bake for a further 30 minutes.

RUSSIAN VEAL BALLS WITH NOODLES
Serves 4

1 large onion
3 tablespoons oil
4oz (100gm) white breadcrumbs
1lb (½ kilo) stewing veal, minced
½ level teaspoon salt
pepper
¼ level teaspoon garlic powder
2–3oz (50–75gm) flour
3oz (75gm) butter
6oz (150gm) mushrooms
¾ pint (375ml) chicken stock
8oz (200gm) noodles
1 carton (5oz or 125gm) soured cream

1. Chop onion finely and cook gently for 2–3 minutes until soft in 1 tablespoon oil in a large saucepan or flameproof casserole.
2. Drain onions, reserving the fat.
3. Mix together in a large bowl onions, breadcrumbs, veal, salt, pepper and garlic powder.
4. Divide mixture into 12 pieces and roll into balls. Coat in flour.
5. Add remaining oil with 1oz (25gm) butter to pan or casserole and fry meat balls for about 5 minutes, until golden brown on all sides. Remove and keep on one side.
6. Slice mushrooms, add to pan or casserole and cook for 2–3 minutes.
7. Add 1oz (25gm) flour and mix thoroughly.
8. Remove pan from heat and gradually stir in stock. Bring to the boil, stirring continuously, until sauce thickens.
9. Return meat balls to pan or casserole and cover with lid. Simmer gently for 15 minutes.
10. Meanwhile, cook noodles in plenty of boiling, salted water for 10–15 minutes, or until tender.
11. Drain well and toss in remaining butter. Put on a warmed serving dish.
12. Stir soured cream into pan containing meat balls and reheat but do not boil it. Adjust seasoning.
13. Serve meat balls with noodles.

BRAISED KIDNEY SUPPER
Serves 4–6

2oz (50gm) butter
8 lamb's kidneys, skinned, cored and cut into pieces
1 onion, chopped
3 tomatoes, skinned and chopped
1oz (25gm) flour
¾ pint (375ml) chicken stock
salt and pepper
1 small bayleaf (optional)
chopped parsley
5oz (125gm) freshly boiled long-grain rice (raw weight)

1. Heat butter and fry kidneys until browned.
2. Remove from pan and fry onion and tomato until tender.
3. Add flour and stir.
4. Add stock and bring to the boil, stirring all the time. Boil for 1 minute.
5. Put the kidneys back into the pan and season well, adding bayleaf, if wished.
6. Simmer for about 20 minutes, until kidneys are tender.
7. Put into a serving dish and sprinkle with the parsley.
8. Serve hot with boiled rice.

SHERRIED KIDNEYS
Serves 4

12 lambs' kidneys
2oz (50gm) butter
1 large onion, finely chopped
1oz (25gm) flour
1 garlic clove
¼ pint (125ml) beef stock
9 tablespoons sherry
1 bayleaf
salt and pepper
1 tablespoon chopped parsley

1. Remove fat and skin from kidneys, then cut in half and remove cores.
2. Melt half the butter in a pan and fry onion slowly until pale brown and soft.
3. Add halved kidneys and cook for 2 minutes on each side until they are just turning brown.
4. Remove onion and kidneys from pan and keep hot.
5. Melt remaining butter in pan, blend in flour and cook for 2 minutes.
6. Add crushed garlic, stock and sherry and blend until smooth.
7. Add bayleaf, salt and pepper. Bring to the boil, stirring, and simmer until sauce has thickened.
8. Return onion and kidneys to pan, cover and simmer for 5 minutes or until kidneys are just cooked.
9. Remove bayleaf and adjust seasoning if necessary.
10. Arrange on a serving dish, pour sauce over and sprinkle with parsley.

LIVER ITALIAN-STYLE
Serves 4

1lb (½ kilo) lamb's liver, thinly sliced
1oz (25gm) flour, seasoned with salt and pepper
1 dessertspoon oil
½oz (12gm) butter
2 large onions, sliced
¼ pint (125ml) stock
2 tablespoons tomato purée
1 garlic clove, crushed
2 teaspoons chopped fresh basil or other similar fresh herb
¼ pint (125ml) single cream
salt and pepper
1 teaspoon chopped parsley

1. Coat liver in seasoned flour.
2. Heat oil and butter in a frying pan, add liver and brown lightly on each side. Remove from pan.
3. Add onion to pan and cook gently until soft.
4. Stir in stock, tomato purée, garlic and basil or other fresh herb. Bring to the boil and return liver to the pan.
5. Cover with lid and simmer slowly for about 25 minutes, until liver is tender.
6. Remove liver from pan and arrange on a serving dish.
7. Stir cream into sauce, season to taste and heat through, but do not boil it.
8. Pour sauce over liver and sprinkle with parsley.
9. Serve with pasta or boiled potatoes.

STUFFED ROAST BACON
Serves 6

2½lb (1¼ kilo) top back bacon,
cut in one piece
4oz (100gm) fresh white
breadcrumbs
2 teaspoons mixed herbs
finely grated rind of 1 lemon
salt and pepper
1 small egg, beaten

1. Bone the bacon and soak
overnight in cold water.
2. Next day, preheat oven to
moderately hot, 400 deg F or gas 6
(200 deg C).
3. Place bacon in a large
saucepan and cover with fresh
cold water.
4. Cover the pan, bring to the
boil and simmer for 40 minutes.
5. Make up the stuffing by mixing
together breadcrumbs, mixed
herbs, lemon rind, salt and pepper.
6. Bind together with egg.
7. Drain bacon from cooking
liquor, remove outside skin and
allow to cool.
8. Spread the stuffing along the
inside of the bacon and roll up.
Secure with skewers and string.
9. Place the bacon in a roasting
tin and cook in centre of oven for
40 minutes.
10. Serve hot or cold.

GAMMON SUPPER
(Illustrated on page 71)
Serves 4

4 thick gammon rashers, about
¾ inch thick
4oz (100gm) demerara sugar
3 teaspoons dry mustard
½ pint (250ml) milk
cornflour

1. Preheat oven to moderate to
moderately hot, 375 deg F or gas 5
(190 deg C).
2. Trim gammon rashers and lay
them in a casserole.
3. Sprinkle over 3oz (75gm) sugar
mixed with mustard.
4. Pour milk over and cover with
a lid or piece of foil. Cook in
centre of oven for 45 minutes.
5. Place gammon on a shallow,
ovenware dish.
6. Thicken sauce with cornflour
and water mixed to a paste.
7. Pour sauce over gammon,
sprinkle with remaining sugar
and put under a hot grill.
8. Garnish with watercress and
serve with a green salad.

HONEYED BACON
Serves 4–6

3½–4lb (1¾–2 kilo) joint collar or
forehock
4 tablespoons clear honey
4 tablespoons sherry

1. Soak bacon joint for 12 hours,
or overnight.
2. Place joint in a large pan,
cover with cold water and bring
to the boil. Simmer for 45–50
minutes.
3. Preheat oven to moderate to
moderately hot, 375 deg F or gas 5
(190 deg C).
4. Remove bacon from pan, cut
string and remove skin carefully
with a sharp knife. Score fat into
diamonds.
5. Place bacon in a roasting tin
and glaze with mixed honey and
sherry.
6. Bake in centre of oven for
45–50 minutes, basting
occasionally with glaze.
7. Serve hot with any remaining
sauce or cold with salad.

CHICKEN GOULASH
Serves 4

4 chicken joints
salt and pepper
1oz (25gm) lard
1 medium onion, skinned and
finely chopped
1 teaspoon paprika
2 teaspoons tomato purée
1 can (8oz or 200gm) tomatoes
chicken stock
1 tablespoon flour
1 carton (¼ pint or 125ml)
natural yogurt

1. Sprinkle chicken with salt and
pepper and fry in lard until golden
brown. Remove from pan.
2. Fry onion until tender. Add
paprika and tomato purée.
3. Strain tomatoes and make
juice up to ½ pint (250ml) with
chicken stock.
4. Stir into the saucepan with
tomatoes. Bring to the boil and
replace the chicken.
5. Cover and cook for 40–45
minutes, until chicken is tender.
6. Place chicken pieces in a
serving dish and keep hot.
7. Blend flour with a little water
and stir into the saucepan. Bring
to the boil and cook for 1 minute,
stirring all the time.
8. Stir in yogurt and pour sauce
over the chicken.

CHICKEN IN MUSHROOM SAUCE
Serves 4

1 tablespoon vegetable oil
1oz (25gm) butter
1 small onion, finely chopped
4 chicken joints
1 can condensed mushroom soup
¼ pint (125ml) milk
2–3 tablespoons cream or top of the milk
1 teaspoon lemon juice

1. Heat oil and butter in a shallow pan with a lid.
2. Fry onion and chicken joints slowly, uncovered, until golden brown, turning from time to time.
3. Mix soup and milk together then pour over the chicken.
4. Cover the pan and simmer gently for 30 minutes, stirring occasionally.
5. Remove lid, stir in the cream or milk and then lemon juice.
6. Serve chicken with cooked mushrooms and green peas.

CHICKEN AND RICE CASSEROLE
Serves 4

4 chicken joints
2oz (50gm) butter
1 onion, sliced
1 can (15oz or 375gm) tomatoes
salt and pepper
6oz (150gm) long-grain rice
1 medium can condensed chicken soup

1. Preheat oven to moderately hot, 400 deg F or gas 6 (200 deg C).
2. Trim chicken joints and brown quickly on all sides in butter. Drain and remove to a casserole.
3. Add onion to the hot butter and fry gently until tender and lightly browned, then remove to casserole with chicken.
4. Pour over tomatoes, salt and pepper, rice and chicken soup.
5. Cover and place in centre of oven for 1 hour. Stir occasionally to prevent rice from sticking.
6. Serve with a salad tossed in French dressing (see Basic recipes, page 100).

TASTY CHICKEN WITH SPAGHETTI
Serves 4

2lb (1 kilo) chicken joints
1oz (25gm) flour, seasoned with salt and pepper
3 tablespoons olive oil
8 small, white onions
4oz (100gm) mushrooms, sliced
1 green pepper, cut in thin strips
1 garlic clove, finely chopped
1 can condensed tomato soup
½ soup can water
2 tablespoons lemon juice or vinegar
1 tablespoon Worcestershire sauce
½ teaspoon thyme
8oz (200gm) freshly boiled spaghetti

1. Dust chicken in seasoned flour.
2. Fry in oil until browned, then remove.
3. Add onions, mushrooms, green pepper and garlic and brown lightly.
4. Blend in all remaining ingredients except spaghetti and replace chicken.
5. Cover and simmer for 30 minutes, stirring occasionally.
6. Serve with spaghetti.

SWEET AND SOUR CHICKEN
Serves 4

4 chicken joints
2oz (50gm) cornflour or flour
1oz (25gm) butter
1 small can concentrated orange juice
1 tablespoon wine vinegar
1 tablespoon brown sugar
1 teaspoon ground ginger
salt and pepper
¾ pint (375ml) chicken stock
1lb (½ kilo) new potatoes, scraped
1 large orange

1. Preheat oven to moderate to moderately hot, 375 deg F or gas 5 (190 deg C).
2. Coat chicken joints in cornflour or flour.
3. Fry until golden, in the butter, then place in a casserole dish.
4. Combine orange juice, vinegar, sugar, ground ginger, salt and pepper with stock, pour over chicken and cover.
6. Cook in centre of oven for 30 minutes.
7. Add potatoes and cook for a further hour.
8. Remove rind and pith from the orange. Cut rind into thin strips and orange flesh into slices and place both on top of chicken 15 minutes before removing from the oven.

CHICKEN IN RED WINE
Serves 4–6

6 chicken joints
1oz (25gm) butter
4oz (100gm) baby onions
4oz (100gm) streaky bacon,
de-rinded and cut into strips
4oz (100gm) button mushrooms
¼ pint (125ml) red Burgundy
wine
½ pint (250ml) chicken stock
1 garlic clove, crushed
(optional)
½ teaspoon dried mixed herbs
salt and pepper
1oz (25gm) butter
1oz (25gm) flour

1. Brown chicken joints in butter
and remove from pan.
2. Brown the onions, add bacon
and mushrooms and fry for a few
minutes.
3. Add wine, stock, garlic, herbs,
salt and pepper and replace the
chicken.
4. Cover and cook gently for 50
minutes, or until the chicken is
tender. Remove chicken and keep
warm.
5. Mix butter with flour and add
to the liquid in small spoonfuls.
6. Bring to the boil and stir until
thickened.
7. Replace chicken and reheat for
3 minutes. Serve hot.

SPANISH CHICKEN
Serves 4

1 chicken, jointed
1oz (25gm) flour, seasoned with
salt and pepper
2oz (50gm) bacon
2oz (50gm) butter or dripping
2 Spanish onions
2 green peppers
1 can (8oz or 200gm) peeled
tomatoes
¼ pint (125ml) sherry or stock
salt and pepper
chopped parsley

1. Dip chicken pieces in seasoned
flour.
2. Dice the bacon and fry it until
cooked, then take it out and add
butter or dripping.
3. Fry chicken until brown, then
put bacon and chicken in a
stewpan or casserole.
4. Add sliced onions, peppers and
tomatoes, sherry or stock and
seasoning. Cover and cook gently
for 30 minutes.
5. Serve chicken garnished with
parsley.

CIDER CHICKEN AND SWEETCORN
(Illustrated on page 71)
Serves 4

4oz (100gm) mushrooms
3oz (75gm) butter
1 chicken, jointed
2oz (50gm) flour, seasoned with
salt and pepper
1 pint (approximately ½ litre)
cider
¼ pint (125ml) cream
salt and pepper
1 large can sweetcorn

1. Preheat oven to hot, 450 deg F
or gas 8 (230 deg C).
2. Chop mushrooms and fry in 1oz
(25gm) butter. Remove from pan.
3. Roll chicken in seasoned flour
and fry in remaining butter until
golden.
4. Place chicken and mushrooms
in a heatproof dish.
5. Boil cider in the frying pan,
stirring with a wooden spoon.
6. Add cream, salt and pepper
and cook for 2 minutes without
boiling.
7. Pour cider sauce over chicken
joints, cover and place in centre
of oven for 30 minutes.
8. Remove chicken to a serving
dish, surround with heated
sweetcorn and pour sauce over.
9. Serve with creamed potatoes.

ORANGE-GLAZED CHICKEN
Serves 4

1 chicken
8oz (200gm) pork sausagemeat
¼ teaspoon ground ginger
1 level tablespoon cornflour
juice of 4 oranges
2oz (50gm) blanched almonds
watercress

1. Preheat oven to moderate, 350
deg F or gas 4 (180 deg C).
2. Stuff the chicken with
sausagemeat and roast for 1½
hours in centre of oven until
tender and golden.
3. Blend together the ginger and
cornflour and add orange juice.
4. Bring to the boil.
5. Put chicken on a serving dish
and pour orange mixture over.
6. Sprinkle with almonds and
garnish with watercress.

SAVOURY CHICKEN SLICE
Serves 4

2 medium onions, chopped
2oz (50gm) butter
8oz (200gm) cottage cheese
1 teaspoon marjoram
2 tablespoons chopped parsley
salt and pepper
1 egg, beaten
8 chicken breasts
8 mushrooms

1. Preheat oven to moderate, 350
deg F or gas 4 (180 deg C).
2. Lightly fry the onion in 1oz
(25gm) butter.
3. Mix together cottage cheese,
onion, marjoram, parsley, salt and
pepper and bind with egg.
4. Flatten out chicken breasts
and spread four with the mixture.
5. Place the other four on top.
Put into an ovenproof dish.
6. Slice the mushrooms over the
top and dot with remaining butter.
7. Cover and cook in centre of
oven for 30 minutes.

ORANGE CHICKEN
Serves 4–6

1 chicken
fat for frying
juice of 2 oranges
chicken stock
1 tablespoon honey
1 tablespoon lemon juice
1 tablespoon cider or wine
vinegar
2 cloves
salt and pepper
1oz (25gm) flour
1 orange, peeled and thinly
sliced

1. Preheat oven to moderate, 350
deg F or gas 4 (180 deg C).
2. Brown the chicken on all sides,
then place in a casserole.
3. Make the orange juice up to ½
pint (250ml) with chicken stock.
4. Stir in the honey, lemon juice,
vinegar, cloves, salt and pepper.
5. Pour over the chicken and
bake in centre of oven for 1½
hours, or until chicken is tender.
6. Pour off the sauce into a pan
and remove the cloves.
7. Blend the flour with a little
water and stir into the sauce.
8. Bring to the boil and simmer
for 1 minute, stirring all the time.
9. Pour over the chicken,
garnish with rind of orange cut
into thin strips and surround with
slices of fruit.

CHICKEN PAPRIKA
Serves 4

grated rind of 1 lemon
4 chicken joints
1 onion, chopped
1 blade of mace
6 peppercorns
sprig of fresh thyme or a pinch
of dried thyme
fresh parsley stalks
salt
1½ pints (approximately ¾ litre)
water
3oz (75gm) butter
4oz (100gm) button mushrooms
1oz (25gm) flour
2 tablespoons paprika
1 carton (5oz or 125gm) soured
cream

1. Place lemon rind, chicken joints, onion, mace, peppercorns, thyme, parsley stalks, salt and water in a large saucepan.
2. Cover and bring to the boil. Simmer for 1–1¼ hours until tender.
3. Remove chicken, strain and reserve 1 pint (approximately ½ litre) stock. Skim of excess fat. Remove meat from bones and cut it into cubes.
4. Melt butter in a large pan or flameproof casserole, fry mushrooms, then remove from pan.
5. Add flour and paprika pepper and cook for a few minutes. Remove pan from heat and slowly add the reserved chicken stock, beating well.
6. Return pan to the heat, bring sauce to the boil and allow to thicken, stirring continuously.
7. Add chicken and mushrooms to pan and heat through.
8. Stir in soured cream, heat but do not boil it. Adjust seasoning.
9. Serve with plain boiled rice or noodles.

CHICKEN SALAD
Serves 4

4 tomatoes, skinned and
chopped
2 sticks celery, chopped
8oz (200gm) chicken, cooked
and diced
6oz (150gm) potatoes, cooked
and diced
8oz (200gm) frozen mixed
vegetables, cooked
4 tablespoons salad oil
2 tablespoons cider or wine
vinegar
1 tablespoon lemon juice
large pinch of caster sugar
salt and pepper
1 lettuce, washed

1. Mix together in a salad bowl tomatoes, celery, chicken, potatoes, and mixed vegetables.
2. Whisk together the oil, vinegar, lemon juice, sugar, salt and pepper, or shake together in a screw-topped jar.
3. Mix the dressing gently with the chicken and vegetables and leave in a cool place until dressing has been absorbed.
4. Line salad bowl with lettuce and arrange salad in the centre.

COD CUTLETS WITH CHEESE
Serves 4

4 cod or haddock cutlets
juice of 1 lemon
salt and pepper
6oz (150gm) cheese, grated
1 tablespoon mixed herbs
1 small onion, finely chopped
2oz (50gm) butter

1. Wash cutlets and dry thoroughly.
2. Squeeze a little lemon juice on each cutlet and season well.
3. Mix cheese, herbs and onion together and add a little lemon juice.
4. Divide mixture into four portions and form each into a firm ball.
5. Place a ball of cheese mixture on each cutlet and dot with butter.
6. Cook under a hot grill until the cutlets are cooked through. Serve piping hot.

GOLDEN HERRING CRISP
Serves 4

4 fresh herrings, boned
2oz (50gm) butter
6oz (150gm) soft brown sugar
1 level teaspoon powdered
mustard
1oz (25gm) walnuts, chopped
1 carton (5oz or 125gm) natural
yogurt
paprika

1. Place herrings on foil in a grill pan and brush with melted butter.
2. Mix brown sugar and mustard together.
3. Sprinkle half the mixture on top of the herrings and grill very slowly for 4–5 minutes.
4. Turn fish over carefully and sprinkle with remaining sugar and mustard.
5. Continue cooking for 3–4 minutes.
6. Lift herrings carefully on to a heated oval serving dish, reserving the fish liquor left in the foil. Keep fish hot.
7. Mix walnuts with yogurt and stir in fish liquor.
8. Spoon on to both ends of serving dish and sprinkle with paprika pepper.

CURRIED HADDOCK
Serves 4

1½oz (37gm) butter
1lb (½ kilo) haddock, skinned
1 onion, finely chopped
1 level dessertspoon curry
powder
¼ teaspoon curry paste
1oz (25gm) flour
½ pint (250ml) stock
1 tablespoon lemon juice
½ pint (250ml) picked shrimps

1. Melt butter in pan.
2. Cut haddock into neat pieces and brown in butter, then remove and keep warm.
3. Add onion to butter and cook until tender but not brown.
4. Mix in curry powder and paste.
5. Add flour and cook for 1 minute.
6. Beat in stock and lemon juice, add shrimps and simmer for 20 minutes.
7. Serve hot.

SAVOURY MINCE LASAGNE
Serves 4

4oz (100gm) lasagne
2 tablespoons corn oil
1 small onion, chopped
1 garlic clove, crushed
1lb (½ kilo) minced beef
1 beef stock cube
1 small can tomato purée
1 medium can tomatoes
1 small green or red pepper,
chopped
dash of Tabasco sauce
¼oz (6gm) cornflour

1. Cook lasagne in boiling, salted water until tender.
2. Heat corn oil and fry onion, garlic and minced beef until golden brown.
3. Add beef stock cube, tomato purée, tomatoes, green or red pepper and Tabasco sauce.
4. Stir until boiling and simmer gently for 15–20 minutes.
5. Blend cornflour with a little cold water, stir into the mixture and cook for 1 minute, stirring all the time.
6. Arrange the drained lasagne in a serving dish and place meat mixture on top.

PIZZA PIE
Serves 4

1oz (25gm) butter
4oz (100gm) self-raising flour
½ level teaspoon baking powder
½ level teaspoon dry mustard
½ level teaspoon salt
1 medium onion, grated
5oz (125gm) cheese, grated
½ level teaspoon mixed herbs
1 egg
1 tablespoon milk
4 tomatoes, peeled and sliced
¼ level teaspoon oregano,
mixed herbs or basil
4–6 stuffed olives, sliced

1. Preheat oven to moderately hot, 400 deg F or gas 6 (200 deg C).
2. Rub butter into sieved dry ingredients until mixture resembles fine breadcrumbs.
3. Add grated onion, 3oz (75gm) cheese and herbs.
4. Mix in egg and milk to form a soft dough. Turn on to a lightly floured board and knead lightly.
5. Shape into a flat round 8–9 inches in diameter and place on a baking sheet.
6. Arrange sliced tomatoes on top.
7. Sprinkle with herbs and remaining cheese and arrange olives on top.
8. Bake in the oven on second shelf from the top for 20–25 minutes. Serve hot, cut into slices.

MUSHROOM AND CHEESE PANCAKES
Serves 4

4½oz (112gm) plain flour
2 eggs
1½oz (37gm) butter, melted
1 tablespoon cooking oil
2oz (50gm) Cheddar cheese,
grated
scant 1 pint (approximately ½
litre) milk and water mixed
1 small onion, chopped
4oz (100gm) mushrooms

1. Preheat oven to moderately hot, 400 deg F or gas 6 (200 deg C).
2. Sift 3½oz (87gm) flour into a bowl.
3. Add eggs, ½oz (12gm) butter, oil and 1½oz (37gm) cheese.
4. Add half the milk and water and beat thoroughly to a smooth mixture.
5. Melt remaining butter in a pan and cook onion until tender.
6. Chop and add mushrooms.
7. Stir in remaining flour and pour in remaining milk and water.
8. Stir until boiling and cook until thickened.
9. Pour pancake mixture, a little at a time, into a hot, greased frying pan. Cook pancakes on both sides until golden.
10. Fill each pancake with mushroom mixture.
Roll up and lay in an ovenware dish.
11. Scatter with remaining cheese and put in centre of oven for 10 minutes.

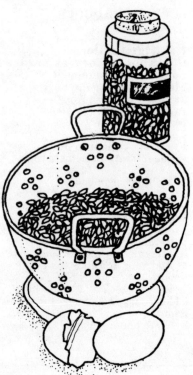

Quick desserts

Desserts, puddings, afters – call them what you will – here is a collection for you to choose from. You'll find all sorts, hot and cold, to suit every occasion.

SUMMER FRUIT SALAD
Serves 4

8oz (200gm) gooseberries
4oz (100gm) redcurrants
4oz (100gm) grapes
5oz (125gm) caster sugar
3 tablespoons water
8oz (200gm) raspberries
cream to serve

1. Top and tail gooseberries and currants.
2. Put into a saucepan with grapes and 4oz (100gm) sugar and the water.
3. Place over a very low heat, until sugar is melted.
4. Stir in the raspberries.
5. Add remaining sugar, chill and serve with a bowl of cream.

FRUIT IN JELLY
Serves 4–6

1 pint (approximately ½ litre) lemon jelly
4oz (100gm) black grapes, halved and pipped
1 banana, sliced
4oz (100gm) cherries, halved and stoned
1 apple, peeled and sliced

1. Set a thin layer of jelly in a patterned mould.
2. Dip pieces of fruit in liquid jelly and arrange in a pattern over the jelly.
3. Allow to set.
4. Cover with another layer of jelly.
5. Repeat layers, until the mould is full. Any leftover jelly can be set separately, chopped and used to decorate.
6. When set, loosen the edges and turn out. Serve with cream, if wished.

FRUIT DESSERT
Serves 4

1 egg white
½ pint (250ml) double cream, whipped
2 small cans strained raspberry, apple and rosehip dessert (baby food range)
flaked almonds to decorate

1. Whisk egg white stiffly and fold into whipped cream.
2. Fold in the raspberry, apple and rosehip dessert and pile into four glasses.
3. Chill and serve decorated with browned, flaked almonds.

HONEY CUSTARD
Serves 4

3 eggs
pinch of salt
6 tablespoons clear honey
1 pint (approximately ½ litre) milk
¼ teaspoon vanilla essence
pinch of nutmeg
canned fruit to serve

1. Preheat oven to moderate, 350 deg F or gas 4 (180 deg C).
2. Lightly beat the eggs, salt and honey together.
3. Heat milk until hot but not boiling and pour on to eggs, stirring all the time.
4. Add vanilla essence.
5. Strain egg and milk into a lightly buttered 1½-pint (approximately ¾ litre) pie dish.
6. Sprinkle with nutmeg.
7. Place pie dish in a shallow roasting tin in ¾ inches cold water and bake in centre of oven for 1 hour, or until set. Serve with canned fruit.

CREME CARAMEL
Serves 4

5oz (125gm) granulated sugar
4 tablespoons water
4 eggs
1 pint (approximately ½ litre)
milk
1 teaspoon vanilla essence

1. Preheat oven to moderate, 350
deg F or gas 4 (180 deg C).
2. Dissolve 4oz (100gm) sugar in
about half the cold water over a
fairly low heat.
3. Bring to the boil without
stirring until syrup is just a
golden brown. (Do not allow it to
become dark brown.)
4. Remove pan from the heat
immediately and add rest of water.
5. Stir well and pour into a hot
straight-sided mould or ovenproof
basin, twisting it so that the
bottom and sides are coated with
caramel.
6. Beat eggs and remaining sugar
together. Heat milk in a pan until
warm but not boiling.
7. Add essence and stir into the
egg mixture.
8. Strain into the mould or basin
and stand it in a pan of warm
water.
9. Bake in centre of oven for
35–40 minutes, until just set.
10. Remove from pan of water.
Do not turn out until completely
cold.

CHOCOLATE CUPS
Serves 4

4oz (100gm) plain chocolate
3 eggs, separated
3 tablespoons sherry or 1
tablespoon brandy
a little chocolate or whipped
cream to decorate

1. Grate chocolate and put it in a
bowl over a pan of hot water.
2. Beat in the egg yolks.
3. Remove from the heat and stir
in the sherry or brandy.
4. Whisk egg whites until stiff
and fold into the mixture.
5. Pour immediately into glasses
and leave to become cold.
6. Serve with melted or grated
chocolate or cream.

ICED RICE AND PEARS
Serves 4

1 large can creamed rice
pudding
1 medium can pears
2–3 tablespoons raspberry or
strawberry jam
a squeeze of lemon juice

1. Share the creamed rice
equally among four individual
serving dishes.
2. Place the drained pear halves
on top of the rice, rounded sides
up.
3. Warm the jam in a saucepan.
4. Add the lemon juice.
5. Spoon over the pears, chill and
serve.

CRUNCHY LEMON PIE
(Illustrated on page 72)
Serves 4–6

4oz (100gm) butter
4oz (100gm) sugar
6oz (150gm) digestive biscuits,
crushed with a rolling pin
1 level tablespoon gelatine
4 tablespoons water
¼ pint (125ml) lemon juice
4 eggs, separated
8oz (200gm) caster sugar
salt
2 teaspoons cornflour
chopped nuts
green food colouring
¼ pint (125ml) double cream,
whipped

1. Melt butter and sugar in a
saucepan.
2. Stir in the biscuit crumbs.
3. Mix well together and press
the mixture into an 8-inch (20cm)
pie plate.
4. Chill until firm.
5. Dissolve gelatine in water over
a low heat.
6. Blend with lemon juice, egg
yolks, half the sugar, the salt and
cornflour.
7. Cook gently over a pan of hot
water until mixture thickens
slightly.
8. Leave in a cool place until
nearly set.
9. Whisk egg whites until stiff
enough to stand in peaks.
10. Add remaining sugar and fold
into the lemon mixture.
11. Spoon into the crumb case
and chill.
12. Mix nuts with a few drops of
green food colouring and sprinkle
them over the pie.
13. Decorate with whipped cream
and serve.

LEMON SOUFFLE
Serves 4–6

1 lemon jelly
grated rind and juice of 1 lemon
1 large can evaporated milk
¼ pint (125ml) double cream
chopped nuts or grated
chocolate to decorate

1. Dissolve jelly in ¼ pint (125ml) hot water, and make up to ½ pint (250ml) with cold water.
2. Add lemon rind and put jelly aside until almost set.
3. Whisk the evaporated milk and strained lemon juice together until it is thick and light.
4. Gradually whisk in the jelly.
5. Continue to whisk until the mixture begins to thicken, then fold in the cream.
6. Pour the mixture into a glass dish.
7. Decorate with nuts or chocolate and chill until quite firm.

GOOSEBERRY CREAM FLAN
Serves 6

5oz (125gm) digestive biscuits
3oz (75gm) butter
1 can (14oz or 350gm) gooseberry pie filling
1½oz (37gm) caster sugar
1 teaspoon lemon juice
½oz (12gm) gelatine
2 tablespoons cold water
½ pint (250ml) double cream

1. Crush biscuits and add to melted butter in a pan.
2. Grease a 7-inch (18cm) cake tin with a removable base and press biscuits firmly in.
3. Purée or sieve the pie filling and add sugar and lemon juice.
4. Dissolve gelatine in water over a pan of hot water. Add to fruit.
5. Whip cream to form soft peaks.
6. Fold fruit purée into cream and blend well. Pour on top of biscuit base and chill till set.

PLUM CRUMBLE
Serves 4–6

1 large can Victoria plums
4oz (100gm) plain flour
3oz (75gm) butter
1oz (25gm) sugar
1oz (25gm) toasted coconut
1 family block dairy ice cream

1. Preheat oven to moderate to moderately hot, 375 deg F or gas 5 (190 deg C).
2. Turn the plums into a pie dish.
3. Sieve the flour into a bowl and rub in 2oz (50gm) butter.
4. Stir in sugar and coconut and put this mixture on top of the plums.
5. Dot with remaining butter and bake in centre of oven for 45 minutes.
6. Serve hot with slices of ice-cream.

STRAWBERRY CREAM LAYERS
Serves 4

½ pint (250ml) double cream
4oz (100gm) cake crumbs
2oz (50gm) almonds, chopped
1oz (25gm) soft brown sugar
1 teaspoon lemon juice
1 can strawberry pie filling
a few whole strawberries, fresh or frozen

1. Whip the cream until just beginning to thicken. Set a little aside for decoration.
2. Blend in cake crumbs, almonds, sugar and lemon juice.
3. Layer this mixture alternately with the pie filling in tall sundae glasses.
4. Finish with a layer of whole strawberries.
5. Decorate with rest of cream and serve chilled.

ICE CREAM SUNDAES
Serves 4

1 can fruit salad
1 small block strawberry ice cream
1 block chocolate or vanilla ice cream
fruit and cream to serve

1. Drain fruit and cut into small pieces.
2. Put 1 spoonful strawberry ice cream in the bottom of each sundae glass.
3. Add 1 spoonful fruit salad, then 1 spoonful chocolate or vanilla ice-cream.
4. Continue in this way and top with fruit and cream.

LOGANBERRY SUNDAE
Serves 4

1 packet plain biscuits
2oz (50gm) butter
2oz (50gm) caster sugar
2 tablespoons treacle
¾ packet raspberry jelly
1 large can evaporated milk
1 large can loganberries
whipped cream to decorate

1. Crumble the biscuits, melt butter and add sugar.
2. Allow sugar to dissolve before adding treacle.
3. Stir the crumbled biscuits into the mixture.
4. Keep stirring until well coated with treacle mixture.
5. Melt jelly in a bowl over hot water.
6. Whisk evaporated milk until it doubles.
7. Add jelly to the milk, whisking continuously.
8. Add a little loganberry juice and some loganberries.
9. Layer the loganberry mousse with the crunchy toffee biscuit mixture.
10. Serve topped with a whirl of whipped cream and the rest of the loganberries.

CINNAMON SLICES
Serves 4

4 slices of stale bread
2 tablespoons jam
½ pint (250ml) pancake batter (see Basic recipes, page 100)
deep fat for frying
1 tablespoon sugar
1 teaspoon ground cinnamon

1. Cut bread into thin strips and remove the crusts.
2. Spread each strip with jam and dip it into batter.
3. Fry in deep fat and when brown, drain and serve sprinkled with sugar and cinnamon.

FRUIT FRITTERS
Serves 4

2oz (50gm) plain flour
¾ teaspoon baking powder
¼ teaspoon salt
1 egg
3 tablespoons cold water
2 teaspoons lemon juice
2 teaspoons olive oil
fruit (apple, banana etc.), thinly sliced
fat for frying
caster sugar

1. Sieve flour, baking powder and salt into a bowl.
2. Beat egg, water and lemon juice with a fork.
3. Make a well in centre of flour and pour in the egg mixture.
4. Beat to a smooth batter, then stir in oil.
5. Coat each piece of fruit in the batter.
6. Fry in hot fat and drain.
7. Dredge with sugar and serve.

QUICK CHARLOTTE RUSSE
Serves 4

½ pint (250ml) double cream
1 egg white
2oz (50gm) icing sugar
1oz (25gm) nuts, chopped
2oz (50gm) glacé cherries, chopped
flavouring (vanilla, almond)
sponge fingers

1. Whip cream until thick.
2. Beat egg white stiffly.
3. Fold in sugar, cream, nuts, cherries and flavouring, reserving a few nuts or cherries for decoration.
4. Spoon mixture into dishes and decorate with nuts or cherries.
5. Serve with sponge fingers.

CHANTILLY STRAWBERRIES
Serves 4–6

1lb (½ kilo) strawberries
¼ pint (125ml) Grand Marnier
2oz (50gm) caster sugar
½ pint (250ml) double cream
2 egg whites
1 sponge flan case

1. Wash, hull and slice the strawberries into a bowl. Drench with Grand Marnier.
2. Sprinkle with sugar and leave in a cold place for 1 hour.
3. Whip the cream until lightly thickened.
4. Whisk the egg whites and fold into the cream with the strawberries and the juice.
5. Pour into sponge flan case and serve immediately.

FROZEN STRAWBERRY CAKE
Serves 4

12oz (300gm) fresh or frozen
strawberries, crushed
12oz (300gm) digestive biscuits,
crushed into crumbs
4 tablespoons clear honey
½ pint (250ml) double cream
½ teaspoon vanilla essence

1. Mix strawberries and biscuit
crumbs together in a basin.
2. Stir in honey, half the cream
and vanilla essence and mix well.
3. Line a freezing tray with
waxed paper and fill with
strawberry mixture.
4. Freeze until firm.
5. Remove paper and cut
strawberry cake into squares.
6. Whip rest of cream until stiff,
pipe a whirl of cream on top of
each square and serve at once.

COFFEE ICE CREAM CUBES
Serves 4–6

Don't attempt this recipe unless
your ice-cream is straight from
the freezer; it must be very firm
to slice into cubes.

1½ teaspoons instant coffee
powder
1½ tablespoons water
3oz (75gm) desiccated coconut,
sweetened
1 family brick rich vanilla
ice cream

1. Blend coffee powder with
water.
2. Add coconut and mix
thoroughly.
3. Cut a family block of ice-cream
into 15 small cubes and sprinkle
with coconut mixture.
4. Serve at once, or refreeze until
needed.

BROWN BREAD ICE CREAM
Serves 4–6

½ pint (250ml) double cream
¼ pint (125ml) single cream
3oz (75gm) sieved icing sugar
4oz (100gm) brown
breadcrumbs (1 day stale)
1 tablespoon rum or rum
flavouring
2 eggs, separated

1. Whisk double cream till just
stiff. Gradually whisk in single
cream. Fold in icing sugar and
crumbs.
2. Mix rum with egg yolks and
fold in.
3. Whisk egg whites till almost
stiff. Fold into mixture. Pour into
freezing trays and freeze till firm
in refrigerator or freezer. (There
is no need to beat during freezing
time.)

ICE CREAM FLAN
Serves 6

4oz (100gm) butter
4oz (100gm) caster sugar
3oz (75gm) drinking chocolate
powder
3 tablespoons cream
vanilla essence
2½oz (62gm) cornflakes
1 block ice cream
8 wafers
¼ pint (125ml) double cream
4 glacé cherries

1. Cream butter and sugar
together.
2. Stir in the drinking chocolate
powder, cream and vanilla
essence to taste.
3. Stir in the lightly crushed
cornflakes.
4. Oil a deep, 7-inch (18cm) pie
plate and press cornflake mixture
round the sides with a spoon.
5. Fill the centre with ice-cream
and decorate with wafers cut into
triangles.
6. Pipe with whipped cream and
top with glacé cherries.

BAKED FRUIT ALASKA
Serves 4

1 family sponge cake
1 family block ice cream
1 can fruit cocktail or stewed
fruit
2 egg whites
4oz (100gm) caster sugar

1. Preheat oven to hot, 450 deg F
or gas 8 (230 deg C).
2. Place cake on a fireproof dish
and put ice cream on top.
3. Pile on some fruit, taking care
it does not slip off.
4. Whisk egg whites until stiff
and fold in almost all the sugar.
5. Coat the Alaska well with
meringue.
6. Sprinkle with remaining sugar
and bake in centre of oven for 4–5
minutes, until lightly coloured.
Serve at once.

COFFEE AND WALNUT SAUCE WITH ICE CREAM
Serves 4–6

½oz (12gm) cornflour
1 level dessertspoon instant
coffee
½ pint (250ml) milk
½oz (12gm) caster sugar
1oz (50gm) walnuts, chopped
1 family block ice cream

1. Blend cornflour and instant
coffee with a little of the milk.
2. Boil the remainder of milk and
pour on to the cornflour mixture.
3. Return to the pan and bring
back to the boil, stirring carefully
all the time.
4. Simmer for about 2 minutes.
5. Add sugar and chopped
walnuts and serve hot on top of
ice cream in individual dishes.

GINGER CREAM PUDDING
Serves 4–6

½ pint (250ml) double cream
1 teaspoon vanilla essence
1 packet ginger biscuits
grated chocolate or chocolate
buttons to decorate

1. Mix whipped cream and vanilla essence together and use half of it to spread one side of the whole biscuits. Pile biscuits on top of each other.
2. Lay the roll of biscuits on its side on a serving dish and cover with remaining cream mixture.
3. Put in refrigerator to chill for at least 3–4 hours so that biscuits soften before serving.
4. Decorate with grated chocolate or chocolate buttons and cut into diagonal slices to serve.

CREAM CROWDIE
Serves 4

4 tablespoons coarse oatmeal
½ pint (250ml) double cream
1oz (25gm) caster sugar
vanilla essence
2 tablespoons raspberries

1. Toast the oatmeal under the grill.
2. Whip cream and stir in oatmeal gradually.
3. Sweeten to taste and flavour with vanilla essence.
4. Stir in the raspberries and serve at once.

GOOSEBERRY WHIP
Serves 4–6

This dessert is equally good in a pastry case, topped with cream.

1lb (½ kilo) gooseberries
3½oz (87gm) granulated sugar
¼ pint (125ml) plus 4
tablespoons warm water
¼ pint (125ml) custard
1 teaspoon lemon juice
¼oz (6gm) gelatine
2 egg whites

1. Stew gooseberries gently with 2oz (50gm) sugar in ¼ pint (125ml) water until fruit is tender.
2. Drain and sieve fruit and add custard, lemon juice and remaining sugar to the purée.
3. Dissolve gelatine in remaining warm water and add to the fruit mixture.
4. Whisk egg whites until stiff, fold into the mixture and chill.
5. Pile into a glass bowl to serve.

BLACKBERRY FLUMMERY
Serves 6

1lb (½ kilo) blackberries
4oz (100gm) water
8oz (200gm) granulated sugar
pinch of salt
pinch of cinnamon
2 tablespoons arrowroot

1. Wash and carefully pick over blackberries.
2. Combine blackberries, water, sugar, salt and cinnamon in a saucepan.
3. Bring mixture to boiling point. Reduce heat and simmer gently until slightly syrupy.
4. Add 3 tablespoons water to arrowroot, stirring to a smooth paste. Blend this into the hot blackberry mixture.
5. Cook until mixture is slightly thickened and translucent. Leave to cool.
6. Serve cold with double cream, if desired.

APRICOT FOOL
Serves 4–6

1lb (½ kilo) fresh apricots
2oz (50gm) caster sugar
2 tablespoons water
2 level dessertspoons custard
powder
1oz (25gm) granulated sugar
½ pint (250ml) milk
¼ pint (125ml) double cream or
evaporated milk
½oz (12gm) angelica diamonds
1oz (25gm) walnuts, chopped

1. Wash apricots and remove stones.
2. Dissolve caster sugar in water over a low heat, add the fruit and simmer gently until tender.
3. Pass through a fine sieve.
4. Mix custard powder and granulated sugar with a little of the cold nilk and put the rest on to boil.
5. Pour on to the blended custard powder, stirring well. Return to pan and bring to the boil, stirring continuously.
6. Cook gently for 1–2 minutes. Allow to cool.
7. Stir into the apricot purée.
8. Lightly whip cream or evaporated milk and fold into the purée.
9. Decorate with angelica diamonds and chopped walnuts.

BRISBANE MERINGUE
Serves 4

1 medium can apricot halves
2 teaspoons clear honey
1oz (25gm) walnuts, chopped
2 egg whites
2oz (50gm) caster sugar

1. Preheat oven to moderately
hot, 400 deg F or gas 6 (200 deg C).
2. Drain apricot halves.
3. Mix honey with walnuts and
arrange apricots, hollow part
upwards, in an ovenware dish.
4. Spoon a little honey and nut
mixture into the hollow of each
apricot half.
5. Whisk the egg whites until
very stiff. Fold in the sugar.
6. Pile on to the fruit and cook
in centre of oven for 15 minutes
until meringue is golden. Serve
hot.

HOT TRIFLE
Serves 4–6

1 can sponge pudding
1 medium can apricots
2 tablespoons sherry
1 pint (approximately ½ litre)
thick custard
½oz (12gm) grated chocolate

1. Preheat oven to moderately
hot, 350 deg F or gas 4 (180 deg C).
2. Remove pudding from the can
and slice into four, horizontally.
3. Cut each round in half.
4. Arrange the pudding around
and in the bottom of an ovenproof
dish.
5. Drain the apricots and pour
the syrup and sherry over the
pudding.
6. Place apricots on the pudding,
reserving a few for decoration.
7. Cover with foil and place in
centre of oven for 45 minutes.
8. Pour thick custard over the
pudding and when a skin forms,
arrange apricots on top.
9. Sprinkle with grated chocolate
and put back into the oven to
melt the chocolate.

PINEAPPLE DESSERT
Serves 4

1 can (8oz or 200gm) pineapple
pieces
1 packet pineapple-flavoured
blancmange
2oz (50gm) sugar
½oz (12gm) butter
1 egg, separated
angelica to decorate

1. Drain juice from pineapple and
make it up to ¾ pint (375ml) with
water.
2. Blend blancmange powder and
sugar with a little of the liquid.
3. Put rest of liquid on to heat.
4. Add to the blancmange powder
return to the pan, bring to the
boil and simmer for 3 minutes,
stirring all the time.
5. Remove from the heat and stir
in the butter and egg yolk.
6. Return to the heat and cook
for a further minute without
boiling.
7. Whisk the egg white until stiff
and fold it lightly into the cooled
mixture.
8. Stir in the pineapple,
reserving a few pieces for
decoration.
9. Serve in individual dishes or
piled into a large glass dish.
Decorated with pieces of
pineapple and angelica.

ZABAGLIONE
Serves 4

3 egg yolks
1oz (25gm) caster sugar
2½ tablespoons Marsala
sponge fingers

1. Put egg yolks in a bowl over a
pan of hot water.
2. Add sugar and Marsala.
3. Increase the heat under pan to
moderate.
4. Whisk egg and sugar mixture
until thick and creamy.
5. Serve warm, in glass goblets,
with sponge fingers.

PEACHES PARISIENNE
Serves 4

4 peaches
4 tablespoons sweet white wine
2oz (50gm) icing sugar
8 sponge fingers
¼ pint (125ml) soured cream or
natural yogurt
1 level tablespoon chocolate
powder

1. Skin, stone and slice the
peaches into four dishes.
2. Sprinkle with wine and icing
sugar.
3. Stand two sponge fingers in
each dish.
4. Spoon in the cream or yogurt
and dust with sifted chocolate
powder.

BAKED PEACHES
Serves 4–6

1 large can peach halves
2oz (50gm) soft brown sugar
1 level teaspoon cinnamon or
ginger
single cream to serve

1. Preheat oven to moderate to moderately hot, 375 deg F or gas 5 (190 deg C).
2. Drain the peaches, setting aside ¼ pint (125ml) juice.
3. Arrange peach halves, cut side up, in a small baking or roasting tin.
4. Pour the juice over them.
5. Mix brown sugar and spices and sprinkle evenly over the peaches.
6. Bake in centre of oven for 15 minutes.
7. Serve hot with single cream.

TIPSY PEACHES
Serves 4

1 can (15oz or 375gm) peach
halves
3oz (75gm) cream cheese
3 digestive biscuits, crumbled
1 tablespoon ground almonds
¼ pint (125ml) white wine or
cider

1. Preheat oven to moderate, 350 deg F or gas 4 (180 deg C).
2. Put peaches in a fireproof dish, hollows upwards.
3. Mix together cheese, biscuits and almonds and place a little in each hollow.
4. Pour wine or cider round the peaches and bake in centre of oven for 10–15 minutes.
5. Serve hot or cold.

RASPBERRY MIST
Serves 4

8oz (200gm) raspberries
½ pint (250ml) double cream
1 egg white
1oz (25gm) caster sugar
4 macaroons

1. Crush all but a cupful of raspberries and sieve them.
2. Whip cream until lightly thickened.
3. Whisk egg white stiffly and fold it lightly into the cream.
4. Gently mix in the raspberries, sugar and crushed macaroons.
5. Pile into tall glasses and layer with reserved fruit. Serve chilled.

RASPBERRY MOUSSE
Serves 4–6

1lb (½ kilo) raspberries
1oz (25gm) cornflour
2 eggs, separated
4oz (100gm) sugar
¾ pint (375ml) milk
½oz (12gm) gelatine
2 tablespoons hot water
1 tablespoon Cointreau or
sherry
few drops of cochineal

1. Put half the raspberries into a pan with a little water, reserving the best for decoration.
2. Cook until tender, rub through a sieve and make the quantity of purée up to ¼ pint (125ml) with water.
3. Mix cornflour, egg yolks and 2oz (50gm) sugar smoothly with a little of the milk.
4. Put rest of milk on to heat.
5. Add the mixed cornflour, stir until boiling and boil for 3 minutes, stirring all the time.
6. Remove from the heat.
7. Dissolve gelatine in hot water and add to the raspberry purée.
8. Stir into the cooked cornflour mixture.
9. Add Cointreau or sherry and a few drops of cochineal.
10. Whisk egg whites with remaining sugar, until stiff. Fold lightly into the mixture.
12. Pour into a 2-pint (approximately 1 litre) mould and leave to set.
13. Turn out and surround with remaining fresh raspberries.

CHOCOLATE MOUSSE
(Illustrated on page 72)
Serves 4

4oz (100gm) milk or plain chocolate
4 eggs, separated
double cream and grated chocolate to decorate

1. Melt chocolate with 4 teaspoons water in a thick saucepan, over a very low heat.
2. Remove from heat and beat in egg yolks.
3. Let mixture cool slightly.
4. Whisk egg whites until soft peaks form. Fold into the chocolate.
5. Pour into individual dishes and leave to set. Decorate with whipped cream and grated chocolate.

APPLE UPSIDE DOWN GINGERBREAD
Serves 4–6

2oz (50gm) butter
4oz (100gm) soft brown sugar
1 level teaspoon cinnamon
3 small apples, peeled and cored
1 packet gingerbread mix
whipped cream and glacé cherries to decorate

1. Grease an 8-inch (20cm) roasting tin with butter.
2. Mix brown sugar with cinnamon and sprinkle in base of pan.
3. Cut apples into rings and arrange in brown sugar mixture.
4. Prepare gingerbread mix as directed on packet, and pour over apple slices.
5. Bake as directed for gingerbread mix.
6. Turn out of tin and, when cold, decorate with whipped cream and cherries to serve.

APPLE AND RAISIN CRISPY
Serves 4

1 can apple pie filling
4oz (100gm) soft brown sugar
4oz (100gm) butter
4oz (100gm) rolled oats
2oz (50gm) raisins

1. Preheat oven to moderate, 350 deg F or gas 4 (180 deg C).
2. Place pie filling in a shallow, fireproof dish.
3. Cream sugar and butter together and mix in rolled oats and raisins. Place this mixture over fruit.
4. Bake in centre of oven for about 30 minutes, then serve with cream or custard.

SWISS APPLE CHARLOTTE
Serves 4

2lb (1 kilo) cooking apples
2oz (50gm) sugar
1½oz (37gm) butter
2 tablespoons golden syrup
½oz (12gm) cornflakes
cream or canned milk

1. Peel, quarter and core apples and cook in a little water until soft, then sieve.
2. Add sugar and spoon into a bowl or individual glasses.
3. Melt butter and syrup in a saucepan and add cornflakes, carefully turning them until evenly covered with syrup.
4. Pour cream or milk over the apple, and pile cornflakes on top.

APPLE CRUNCH
Serves 4

2lb (1 kilo) cooking apples
1 teaspoon ground cinnamon
4oz (100gm) sugar
1oz (25gm) cornflakes
4oz (100gm) butter, melted

1. Preheat oven to very moderate, 325 deg F or gas 3 (170 deg C).
2. Peel apples, slice thinly and sprinkle with cinnamon.
3. Mix sugar and cornflakes together, add butter and stir into apples.
4. Put in a fireproof dish and bake in centre of oven until apples are tender and top brown.

CHOCOLATE APPLE PUDDING
Serves 4–6

1½lb (¾ kilo) cooking apples
2 tablespoons water
1 orange
2oz (50gm) granulated sugar
4oz (100gm) butter
4½oz (112gm) caster sugar
2 eggs
6oz (150gm) self-raising flour
1oz (25gm) cocoa
little warm water to mix
cream or custard to serve

1. Preheat oven to moderate to moderately hot, 375 deg F or gas 5 (190 deg C).
2. Peel, core and slice the apples.
3. Add water and simmer gently.
4. Grate orange rind and add to apples with orange juice.
5. When apples are tender, add granulated sugar and turn into an ovenproof dish.
6. Cream together butter and 4oz (100gm) caster sugar until light and fluffy.
7. Beat in lightly whisked eggs, one at a time.
8. Fold in the sieved flour and cocoa with sufficient warm water to give a dropping consistency.
9. Spread evenly over the cooked apples.
10. Bake in centre of oven for 35–40 minutes.
11. Sprinkle with remaining caster sugar and serve with cream or custard.

APPLE SNOW
Serves 4

1lb (½ kilo) cooking apples
juice of half a lemon
½oz (12gm) butter
2oz (50gm) sugar
4 individual sponge cakes
½ pint (250ml) custard
2 egg whites
cream and glacé cherries to decorate

1. Peel, core and slice the apples.
2. Put into a pan with lemon juice, butter and sugar.
3. Cook slowly to a pulp.
4. Leave to cool in a bowl of cold water.
5. Cut sponge cakes into slices and put them in a glass dish.
6. Pour the custard over.
7. Whisk the egg whites until stiff, then gradually whisk in the cold apple mixture.
8. Pile into the dish and decorate with cream and cherries.

MANDARIN-TOPPED PUDDING
Serves 4

1 can marmalade sponge pudding
1 small can mandarin oranges
2 teaspoons arrowroot
orange food colouring

1. Place the pudding in its can in boiling water for 40 minutes.
2. Strain the juice from mandarin oranges into a small saucepan.
3. Blend arrowroot with a little water and add to the mandarin juice.
4. Bring slowly to the boil, stirring occasionally.
5. Reduce the heat and simmer for 3 minutes.
6. Add a few drops of orange food colouring to the sauce and fold in the mandarins. Cover and keep warm.
7. Remove the pudding from the can, following instructions on the can carefully, and place on a hot serving dish.
8. Decorate the top and base of the pudding with the mandarin oranges.
9. Pour sauce over the pudding and serve immediately.

GRILLED ORANGES
Serves 4

4 oranges
2oz (50gm) sugar
2 teaspoons brandy or rum
1oz (25gm) butter

1. Skin, slice and arrange oranges in a fireproof dish.
2. Sprinkle liberally with sugar and brandy or rum.
3. Add knobs of butter and grill until golden.

ORANGE CREAMS
Serves 4–6

6oz (150gm) sugar
1oz (25gm) cornflour
pinch of salt
2 egg yolks
grated rind of half an orange
1 tablespoon lemon juice
juice of 1 orange made up to ½ pint (250ml) with water
½oz (12gm) butter
¼ pint (125ml) double cream
2oz (50gm) plain chocolate, grated

1. Blend the sugar, cornflour, salt, egg yolks, orange rind and lemon juice.
2. Put orange juice and water on to heat with the butter and bring to the boil.
3. Add cornflour mixture and cook for 3 minutes, stirring constantly.
4. Leave until cold, the whisk well.
5. Whisk the cream until thick and fold lightly into orange mixture.
6. Pile into individual dishes and decorate with grated chocolate.

APPLE CREAMS
Serves 4

1 medium can sweetened apple purée
3 level tablespoons soft brown sugar
½ pint (250ml) double cream
toasted almonds to decorate

1. Spoon the apple purée into a basin and stir in the brown sugar.
2. Whip the cream until stiff and fold into the apple mixture.
3. Divide among four individual serving dishes and sprinkle with almonds.
4. Chill before serving.

CHOCOLATE CREAMS
Serves 4–5

4oz (100gm) plain chocolate
2oz (50gm) butter
1oz (25gm) golden syrup
1 teaspoon instant coffee
3 tablespoons single cream
4 tablespoons orange juice
2 tablespoons Cointreau
1 egg white
4 tablespoons whipped cream
4–5 chocolate buttons

1. Break the chocolate into a basin over hot water.
2. Add butter, syrup and coffee and stir until melted.
3. Beat in the cream and orange juice.
4. Remove from heat and whisk occasionally.
5. Stir in Cointreau and lightly fold in the stiffly whisked egg white.
6. Turn into four or five glass dishes and leave to set for a few minutes.
7. Decorate each with a whirl of whipped cream and a chocolate button.

CHERRY TRIFLE
Serves 4

1 jam Swiss roll
2 tablespoons sherry
2oz (50gm) flaked almonds, browned
2 eggs
1oz (25gm) caster sugar
½ pint (250ml) milk
1 can cherry pie filling
whipped cream to decorate

1. Slice the Swiss roll and line a glass dish.
2. Pour sherry and almonds over the Swiss roll slices and allow to stand for 5 minutes.
3. Beat eggs and sugar together in a bowl, add milk and place over a saucepan of hot water.
4. Stir until mixture thickens. Allow to cool slightly.
5. Pour the cherry pie filling over the Swiss roll.
6. Pour the custard on to the cherries.
7. Allow to set and decorate with whipped cream.

CHERRIES FLAMBE
Serves 4–6

4oz (100gm) sugar
¼ pint (125ml) hot water
1lb (½ kilo) cherries
1oz (25gm) butter
1 family brick dairy ice cream
4 tablespoons brandy
½oz (12gm) cornflour

1. Dissolve sugar in hot water and simmer cherries over a low heat until tender but still whole.
2. Drain off the syrup.
3. Heat butter in a pan and add cherries.
4. Toss for a few minutes until well heated through.
5. Set ice cream on a plate.
6. Warm brandy very gently in a pan.
7. Pour over the cherries, set alight and pour them over the ice-cream immediately.
8. Serve at once with the cherry syrup, thickened with cornflour.

CHERRY AND APRICOT FLAMBE
Serves 4–6

2oz (50gm) redcurrant jelly
1 large can apricot halves
1 can black cherries
¼ pint (125ml) brandy (optional)
½oz (12gm) almonds, blanched and split

1. Put redcurrant jelly in a pan.
2. Allow to melt slowly with 4 tablespoons apricot juice.
3. Add drained apricots and cherries and warm the brandy carefully (if used), taking care not to overheat it.
4. Scatter the fruit with almonds and pour brandy over.
5. Ignite and serve at once.

HOT CHERRY COBBLER
Serves 4

1lb (½ kilo) cherries, stewed
2oz (50gm) butter
4oz (100gm) self-raising flour
1½oz (37gm) sugar
1 egg
milk to mix
2oz (50gm) walnuts, chopped
1 carton yogurt

1. Preheat oven to moderately hot, 400 deg F or gas 6 (200 deg C).
2. Drain off excess juice from the cherries and turn them into a pie dish.
3. Rub butter into the flour and add sugar.
4. Mix to a soft dropping consistency with egg and milk.
5. Spread mixture over the fruit.
6. Sprinkle with chopped walnuts and bake for 35 minutes in centre of oven.
7. Serve hot with yogurt.

CHERRY CHEESE CAKE
Serves 4–6

4oz (100gm) butter
6oz (150gm) digestive biscuits, crushed
8oz (200gm) cream cheese
½ pint (250ml) double cream
½ teaspoon lemon juice
1 can cherry pie filling

1. Melt butter in a saucepan, add biscuits and mix well.
2. Line a 7-inch (18cm) pie plate with the biscuit mix and place in a refrigerator for 15 minutes.
3. Cream together cheese and double cream and beat until thick.
4. Add lemon juice.
5. Place in the biscuit crust.
6. Spoon cherry pie filling round edge of flan.

FLAN AUX POMMES
(Illustrated on page 72)
Serves 4–6

shortcrust pastry made with 4oz (100gm) flour (see Basic recipes, page 100)
1lb (½ kilo) cooking apples
¼ pint (125ml) white wine
2 tablespoons water
2oz (50gm) sugar
2 eating apples
juice of 1 lemon
1 glacé cherry

1. Preheat oven to moderately hot, 400 deg F or gas 6 (200 deg C).
2. Roll out and line a 7½-inch (19cm) flan ring with pastry.
3. Prick the base, cover with greaseproof and fill with a handful of dry beans.
4. Bake on second shelf from the top of oven for 15 minutes. Remove beans and paper.
5. Peel and slice cooking apples into a pan.
6. Add wine, water and sugar and cook slowly until tender.
7. Drain and spoon into pastry cases.
8. Core and slice eating apples and dip in lemon juice.
9. Arrange over the top of the flan.
10. Return to the oven for a further 5 minutes.
11. Decorate with a glacé cherry in the centre and serve hot or cold.

WALNUT AND PEAR TART
Serves 4–6

12oz (300gm) plain flour
6oz (150gm) caster sugar
3oz (75gm) walnuts, finely chopped
3 egg yolks
1 level teaspoon cinnamon
2oz (50gm) butter
3oz (75gm) lard
1½ tablespoons iced water
4 pears
¼ pint (125ml) double cream, whipped

1. Preheat oven to moderate to moderately hot, 375 deg F or gas 5 (190 deg C).
2. Sift flour into a circle on a cool surface.
3. Sprinkle 5oz (125gm) sugar over the flour with the walnuts.
4. Blend together the egg yolks, cinnamon, butter, lard and water.
5. Pour this mixture into the centre of the ring of flour.
6. Blend in the flour with the fingertips only and knead into a smooth dough.
7. Wrap in polythene and leave in a cold place for 30 minutes.
8. Roll out and use half to line a 7-inch (18cm) pie plate.
8. Fill the pie with the peeled, halved pears and cover with rest of pastry.
9. Make a hole in the centre of the pie so that the pears can be seen through it.
10. Brush the pastry with water and sprinkle with remaining sugar.
11. Bake in centre of oven for 20 minutes. Serve hot or cold with whipped cream.

QUICK FRUITED TARTS
Makes 8

8 thin arrowroot biscuits
2oz (50gm) cream cheese
1 medium can cherries
4oz (100gm) redcurrant jelly
¼ pint (125ml) canned cream,
whipped

1. Spread biscuits with cheese.
2. Drain cherries and arrange on
the cheese.
3. Melt redcurrant jelly and use
to glaze the fruit.
4. Top with a whirl of whipped
cream.

APRICOT SUZETTES
Serves 4–6

1 pint (approximately ½ litre)
pancake batter (see Basic
recipes, page 100)
1 can apricot pie filling
½ glass sherry

1. Make pancakes and stack them
on an upturned plate. Take each
one and spread with 1 tablespoon
pie filling and fold into four.
2. Put remainder of the can of pie
filling into a frying pan with
sherry. Bring to the boil.
3. Replace folded pancakes in this
mixture and heat through. Serve
immediately.

HONEY CHERRY PANCAKES
Serves 4–6

½ pint (250ml) pancake batter
(see Basic recipes, page 100)
a little oil for frying
1 can (15oz or 375gm) red
cherries
1 level tablespoon cornflour
just under ½ pint (250ml) water
4 tablespoons clear honey
few drops of red food colouring

1. Grease a 7-inch (18cm) frying
pan with oil and make pancakes
in the usual way, browning them
well on each side.
2. Drain and wipe clean the frying
pan. Fold each pancake into four
and arrange them overlapping in
the frying pan.
3. Drain the cherries, reserving
the juice, and remove the stones.
4. Mix cornflour to a smooth
paste with a little cold water.
5. Boil the cherry juice, water
and honey together and pour on
to the cornflour.
6. Return to the pan and bring to
the boil, stirring all the time.
7. Colour pale pink with red
colouring and add the cherries to
the sauce.
8. Pour over the pancakes and
heat gently until heated through.

CHERRY OMELETTE
Serves 2–4

3 eggs, separated
3 tablespoons milk and water
mixed
½oz (12gm) butter
4oz (100gm) cherries, stoned
1oz (25gm) icing sugar
2 tablespoons maraschino
cream to serve

1. Cream egg yolks together
thoroughly, add the milk and
water and whisk again.
2. Whisk egg whites very stiffly
and fold gently into yolk mixture.
3. Melt butter in an omelette pan
without allowing it to brown.
4. Pour egg mixture into omelette
pan and stir well until omelette
begins to set.
5. Cook over a moderate heat
until just turning golden brown
on underside.
6. Put pan quickly under a very
hot grill until top of omelette is
lightly browned.
7. Fill with cherries and sprinkle
with sugar and maraschino.
8. Fold in half and serve at once
on a hot plate, with cream.

PINEAPPLE OMELETTE
Serves 2–4

2 tablespoons water
½oz (12gm) granulated sugar
juice of half a lemon
1 teaspoon rum (optional)
1 small can crushed pineapple, drained
4 eggs
1oz (25gm) caster sugar
½ teaspoon vanilla essence
pinch of salt
1oz (25gm) butter

1. Preheat oven to moderate, 350 deg F or gas 4 (180 deg C).
2. Heat water with granulated sugar, lemon juice and rum, if used.
3. Cook for 2–3 minutes, then mix in drained pineapple.
4. Separate the eggs and whisk yolks with caster sugar in a basin over hot water until thick and creamy.
5. Add vanilla essence and fold in lightly.
6. Whisk egg whites with salt until very stiff and fold into the yolks.
7. Heat half the butter in an 8-inch (20cm) omelette pan and pour in half the egg mixture.
8. Cook the omelette for 1 minute, stirring a few times.
9. Transfer pan to the second shelf down of oven for 8–10 minutes.
10. Spread with some of the pineapple filling and fold in half.
11. Repeat the procedure with remaining butter, egg mixture, and filling to make a second omelette.
12. Serve the omelettes immediately.

PINEAPPLE FRITTERS
Serves 4–6

1 large can pineapple rings, drained
¼ pint (125ml) pancake batter (see Basic recipes, page 100)
oil for deep frying
caster sugar

1. Dip fruit in batter, then lower into fat. Do not crowd the pan or use a frying basket.
2. When crisp and golden, remove with a perforated spoon or a pair of tongs and drain on kitchen paper.
3. Serve immediately, dusted with caster sugar.

SHERRY-BAKED BANANAS
(Illustrated on page 72)
Serves 4

6 bananas, preferably soft
¼ pint (125ml) medium sherry
3oz (75gm) demerara sugar
¾oz (18gm) butter
whipped cream and sponge fingers to serve

1. Preheat oven to moderate to moderately hot, 375 deg F or gas 5 (190 deg C).
2. Peel bananas, cut in half down the centre and place in a shallow, ovenproof dish.
3. Pour sherry over, sprinkle with sugar and dot with butter.
4. Bake in centre of oven for 25 minutes.
5. Serve piping hot with whipped cream and sponge fingers.

CHOCOLATE BANANAS
Serves 4

2 individual sponge cakes, broken up
2 tablespoons sherry
2 bananas
2oz (50gm) chocolate
chopped browned almonds

1. Put cakes in the base of a glass dish.
2. Soak with sherry.
3. Slice the bananas and put on the sponge cake.
4. Pour melted chocolate over and decorate with chopped nuts.

BANANA SPLIT
Serves 4

4 bananas
1 block ice cream
2oz (50gm) plain chocolate
1oz (25gm) chopped nuts

1. Split the bananas in half lengthways and put into four dishes.
2. Put a good spoonful of ice cream on each.
3. Cover with melted chocolate and sprinkle with nuts.

BANANA CUSTARD TART
Serves 4–6

shortcrust pastry made with 6oz (150gm) flour (see Basic recipes, page 100)
3 bananas
1 can ready-made custard

1. Preheat oven to moderate to moderately hot, 375 deg F or gas 5 (190 deg C).
2. Line an 8-inch (20cm) pie plate with pastry and place on a baking tin.
3. Line the pastry with greaseproof paper and fill with baking beans.
4. Bake in the centre of the oven for 10 minutes.
5. Carefully lift out the paper and beans and return to the oven for a further 5 minutes.
6. Leave to cool slightly.
7. Fill with sliced bananas and pour heated custard over.
8. Serve hot or cold.

BANANA BAVAROIS
Serves 4

1 packet vanilla blancmange powder
1oz (25gm) sugar
¾ pint (375ml) milk
2 bananas, sieved
juice of half a lemon
1 small can evaporated milk, chilled
2oz (50gm) chocolate

1. Blend blancmange powder to a smooth cream with sugar and a little milk.
2. Heat the remainder of the milk and pour on to the mixed blancmange powder, stirring well.
3. Return to heat, bring to the boil, boil for 1 minute, stirring all the time.
4. Remove from the heat and stir in the sieved bananas and a squeeze of lemon juice.
5. Add a squeeze of lemon juice to the evaporated milk and whisk until it has the consistency of double cream.
6. Fold into the banana mixture.
7. Pile into glass dishes, chill and serve decorated with grated chocolate.

GOLDEN BANANA AND PINEAPPLE
Serves 4

2oz (50gm) butter
3 bananas
1 medium can pineapple chunks, drained
2oz (50gm) soft brown sugar
¼ level teaspoon ground cinnamon
single cream or ice cream to serve

1. Melt butter in a frying pan over a low heat.
2. Peel bananas, cut into 1-inch chunks and add to the butter.
3. Add drained pineapple.
4. Sprinkle mixed brown sugar and cinnamon over and cook gently over a low heat for about 5 minutes, turning the fruit occasionally. (Keep the heat low, or the sugar may burn.)
5. Serve immediately with cream or ice cream.

BANANAS AND YOGURT
Serves 4

3 bananas
1 carton natural yogurt
2oz (50gm) caster sugar
juice of half a lemon
¼ pint (125ml) double cream
chopped walnuts to decorate

1. Mash bananas in a small bowl, add the yogurt, sugar and lemon juice and whisk together.
2. Whisk the cream until thick and fold into the mixture.
3. Spoon into 4 individual serving dishes.
4. Sprinkle with chopped walnuts and chill.

BANANA-APPLE PUDDING
Serves 4

3 dessert apples
2oz (50gm) soft brown sugar
2 bananas
½oz (12gm) butter
1 large block ice cream

1. Preheat oven to moderately hot, 400 deg F or gas 6 (200 deg C).
2. Peel, core and thinly slice the apples and place half the slices in a small casserole.
3. Sprinkle with half the sugar.
4. Peel and slice the bananas and place them on top of the apple.
5. Top with remaining apple slices.
6. Sprinkle with remaining sugar and dot with butter.
7. Bake for 20 minutes then remove the lid and cook for a further 15–20 minutes, until the apples are cooked.
8. Serve hot, with ice cream.

Basic recipes

FRENCH DRESSING

4 tablespoons olive oil
½ level teaspoon salt
¼ level teaspoon caster sugar
½ level teaspoon freshly
ground pepper
2 tablespoons white wine
vinegar

1. Put oil into a basin and add salt, sugar and pepper.
2. Whisk in the vinegar drop by drop and continue beating until mixture thickens slightly.

Variations
Add a few chopped fresh herbs, a little crushed garlic or a dash of mustard etc.

ASPIC JELLY
Makes ½ pint or 250ml

½oz (12gm) gelatine
½ pint (250ml) boiling water
¼oz (6gm) caster sugar
½ level teaspoon salt
2 tablespoons tarragon vinegar
2 tablespoons lemon juice

1. Dissolve gelatine in boiling water. Add all other ingredients.
2. Leave to cool and thicken.
3. Use as required either before or after it has set as the recipe demands.

Note
Alternatively, thicken a can of consommé with approximately 2 teaspoons gelatine. Or dilute clear meat extract or a bouillon cube with ½ pint (250ml) water and add approximately 2 teaspoons gelatine.

WHITE SAUCE
Makes ½ pint or 250ml

½oz (12gm) butter or margarine
½oz (12gm) flour
½ pint (250ml) cold milk (or milk and stock or water mixed)
salt and pepper

1. Melt the butter or margarine in a pan over a gentle heat.
2. Stir in flour and cook without browning for 2 minutes, stirring all the time.
3. Remove pan from heat and gradually beat in the liquid. Alternatively, add all the liquid and whisk thoroughly.
4. Return to heat and bring to boil, stirring well. Simmer gently for 2–3 minutes and add seasoning. If sauce is to be kept, cover it with greaseproof paper or foil to prevent a skin forming.

THICK WHITE SAUCE
Makes ½ pint or 250ml

Make exactly as for white sauce, above, but double the quantities of butter or margarine and flour used.

CHEESE SAUCE
Makes ½ pint or 250ml

Make up ½ pint (250ml) white sauce (see this page). After sauce has come to the boil and thickened, add 2–4oz (50–100gm) grated cheese and ½ level teaspoon mustard. Stir sauce over low heat until cheese melts.

SHORTCRUST PASTRY
Makes 8oz or 200gm pastry

8oz (200gm) plain flour
1 level teaspoon salt
2oz (50gm) lard
2oz (50gm) butter or margarine
cold water to mix

1. Sift flour and salt into a bowl.
2. Cut fats into flour with a knife.
3. Rub fats into flour with fingertips until mixture resembles fine breadcrumbs.
4. Add water little by little, stirring with a knife until mixture forms large lumps.
5. Bring mixture together with fingertips and knead lightly into a ball.
6. Roll out briskly on a floured board. Avoid stretching the pastry.

Note
Baking temperature: moderately hot, 400 deg F or gas 6 (200 deg C).

RICH SHORTCRUST PASTRY

Make as for shortcrust pastry, above, but sift the flour with ½oz (12gm) icing sugar and mix in 1 egg before adding the water.

Note
Baking temperature: moderate to moderately hot, 375 deg F or gas 5 (190 deg C).

CHEESE PASTRY
Makes 8oz or 200gm pastry

Use for savoury pies, canapé bases, cheese straws and savoury flans.

8oz (200gm) self-raising flour
1 level teaspoon salt
pinch of cayenne pepper
2oz (50gm) lard
2oz (50gm) butter or margarine
5oz (125gm) cheese, grated
1–2 egg yolks
cold water to mix

1. Sift flour, salt and pepper into a bowl.
2. Cut fats into flour with a knife.
3. Rub fats into flour with fingertips until mixture resembles fine breadcrumbs. Add cheese.
4. Mix in egg, then add water little by little, stirring with a knife until mixture forms large lumps.
5. Bring mixture together with fingertips and knead lightly into a ball.
6. Roll out briskly on a floured board. Avoid stretching the pastry.

Note
Baking temperature: moderate, 350 deg F or gas 4 (180 deg C).

SUET CRUST PASTRY
Makes 8oz or 200gm pastry

Use for steak and kidney puddings, sweet puddings and roly polies.

8oz (200gm) self-raising flour or
8oz (200gm) plain flour plus 2
teaspoons baking powder
1 level teaspoon salt
4oz (100gm) beef or mutton
suet, shredded or grated
¼ pint (125ml) cold water

1. Sift self-raising flour (or plain flour and baking powder) into a bowl with salt.
2. Add suet then mix in water with a knife until lumps begin to form.
3. Gather mixture lightly together and knead until smooth.
4. Turn out on a floured board and shape into a ball. Leave to stand 10 minutes before using.

Note
Baking temperature: moderately hot, 400 deg F or gas 6 (200 deg C). Alternatively, steam.

FLAKY PASTRY
Makes 8oz or 200gm pastry

Use for pies, vanilla slices, sausage rolls.

8oz (200gm) plain flour
1 level teaspoon salt
3oz (75gm) lard
3oz (75gm) butter or margarine
1 teaspoon lemon juice
water to mix

1. Sift flour and salt into a bowl. Blend the fats on a plate and mark into four portions.
2. Rub one portion into the flour until it resembles fine breadcrumbs.
3. Mix to a smooth dough with lemon juice and water.
4. Knead dough lightly and roll it out on a floured surface into an oblong.
5. Dot two-thirds of the pastry with second portion of fat.
6. Fold the bottom third up and the top third over into an envelope shape.
7. Allow pastry to relax for 10 minutes in a cold place. This is especially important in warm weather.
8. Repeat the whole process until all the fat is used up.
9. Fold pastry in two, roll out to ¼–½ inch thick and use as required.

Note
Baking temperature: hot, 425 deg F or gas 7 (220 deg C).

PUFF PASTRY
Makes 8oz or 200gm pastry

Use for vol au vents, bouchée cases, patties, mille feuilles, palmiers. It is essential to keep everything including hands very cold for this pastry.

8oz (200gm) plain flour
½ level teaspoon salt
8oz (200gm) unsalted butter in a block or 4oz (100gm) cooking fat and 4oz (100gm) margarine mashed and formed into a block
2 teaspoons lemon juice
6–8 tablespoons very cold water

1. Sift flour and salt into a bowl.
2. Chill the fat if soft. Rub ½oz (12gm) fat into flour.
3. Mix to a dough with lemon juice and water.
4. Roll out dough to twice the length of the block of fat. Place fat on dough and fold dough down over it, sealing edges well with a rolling pin.
5. Give pastry one half turn and roll gently out into a long strip.
6. Fold dough in three, envelope style, and leave, covered, in a cold place for 30 minutes.
7. Repeat turning, rolling and folding six times.
8. Leave pastry to relax for 30 minutes between rollings and before use.

Note
Baking temperature: hot, 450 deg F or gas 8 (230 deg C).

PANCAKE BATTER
Makes ½ pint or 250ml

4oz (100gm) plain flour
pinch of salt
1 egg
½ pint (250ml) cold milk
1 tablespoon oil

1. Sift flour and salt into a bowl.
2. Make a well in the centre and break egg into it.
3. Gradually beat in half the milk and continue beating until batter is smooth.
4. Fold in rest of milk with oil.

Index